Treasures from Royal Collection

The Queen's Gallery
Buckingham Palace

Catalogue published for the exhibition
Treasures from the Royal Collection
at The Queen's Gallery, Buckingham Palace,
1988–9.

Times of opening:
Tuesday–Saturday 10.30am–5pm
Sunday 2–5pm
The exhibition is closed on Monday,
but open on Bank Holidays.
Telephone 01-930 4832

© Her Majesty Queen Elizabeth II, 1988

ISBN 0 9513373 0 0

Designed by Graham Johnson

Printed by Balding + Mansell UK Limited

Contents

Colour Plates

Introduction

On 13 September 1940 a German bomb fell on Buckingham Palace and destroyed the Private Chapel which had been constructed for Queen Victoria, early in her reign, within one of the conservatories placed by John Nash on the west front of the palace. Phoenix-like, however, the Private Chapel rose from its ashes as The Queen's Gallery, opened to the public on 25 July 1962.

The creation of an art gallery on the ruins of the old Private Chapel had been suggested originally by The Queen and The Duke of Edinburgh in order that works of art from all parts of the Royal Collection could be shown to the public in a succession of special exhibitions.

The exhibition with which the Gallery opened was entitled *Treasures from The Royal Collection*. To commemorate the Gallery's Silver Jubilee an exhibition has been mounted which again lays before the public a selection of the most celebrated and beautiful works of art in the Royal Collection. A number of the most famous may also be among the least familiar. The Queen and The Duke of Edinburgh have always considered that the Gallery has an important function in displaying works of art which may not normally be on view to the public.

An exhibition composed solely of works chosen for their beauty cannot present a balanced survey of the Royal Collection or its growth. The selection of paintings became inevitably a tribute to those royal collectors who took most pleasure in the sheer beauty of paint – Charles I, Frederick, Prince of Wales, and George IV – to those who had flair and good taste – Charles II and George III – and to Prince Albert who would have made a conscientious Director of the National Gallery. Many of the pictures in the exhibition have been cleaned and restored for the occasion. The appearance of, for example, the Mabuse (No.2), the Cranach (No.41), the Carracci (No.10) and the Claude (No.21) will certainly prompt fresh awareness of their beauty; and the restoration of the Dürer (No.40), the Metsys (No.43), the Duccio (No.49), the De Hooch (No.23) and, perhaps above all, the Bruegel (No.4) will stimulate revised assessments of these great works.

The choice of the decorative arts has been inevitably restricted by considerations of space; but the works of art illustrate, if only in part and in microcosm, the taste of those royal connoisseurs who made the most distinguished contributions to the collections: Henry VIII, who in 1517 established the Royal Armouries at Greenwich; William III, who admired the work of the expatriate Frenchman, Gerrit Jensen (No.94), and Mary II, who had a passion for pottery and porcelain (No.93); Frederick, Prince of Wales, and his daughter-in-law, Queen Charlotte, who shared a liking for the rococo in (respectively) silver-gilt (Nos.114-19) and porcelain

(Nos. 111–12); George III, a practical man whose principal interest lay in clocks; and George IV, without question the greatest royal collector of the decorative arts, with an eye for English furniture of high quality as well as for French furniture and works of art. Particularly spectacular as evidence of his sustained enthusiasm and discernment are the examples with which he enriched his collections near the end of his life: the De Hooch (No.23), for instance, the *Farm at Laeken* (No.19), the Claude (No.21) and two masterpieces by J.-H. Riesener, the roll-top desk (No.108) and the jewel cabinet (No.103) made for the comtesse de Provence which, as the most magnificent piece of furniture in The Queen's collection, has been placed to catch the eye of every visitor who comes into the Gallery.[1]

A recent exhibition in The Queen's Gallery was devoted to portraits of Kings and Queens. The iconographical element in the Royal Collection has been, in selecting works for the present exhibition, deliberately underplayed. One exception has been made. Because, after his execution, so many of his finest pictures were sold, it is impossible to do justice to Charles I, that legendary figure in the history of royal taste; but it is appropriate that his should be the only portrait to be included in, indeed to preside over, an exhibition of treasures from the collection which he did so much to transform during a short period in its history. As a result of an earlier and even more disastrous fire than the one at Hampton Court in 1986, it is not possible to set beside the triple portrait by Van Dyck the marble bust of the King by Bernini which, in a spectacular fashion, would have symbolized his achievement. The Van Dyck, it should be remembered, was secured by George IV.

---

[1]George IV's achievement as collector and patron will be illustrated in much more detail in a forthcoming exhibition in The Queen's Gallery, devoted to the building, decoration and furnishing of Carlton House.

Abbreviations

Burl. Mag.	*The Burlington Magazine*
Campbell	Lorne Campbell, *The Early Flemish Pictures in the Collection of H.M. The Queen* (1985)
Clifford Smith	H. Clifford Smith, *Buckingham Palace: Its Furniture Decoration & History* (1931)
DOEFM	*Dictionary of English Furniture Makers 1660–1840*, ed. G. Beard and C. Gilbert (1986)
Foskett, N.P.G.	D. Foskett and others, *Samuel Cooper and his contemporaries*, National Portrait Gallery (1974)
FHS	Journal of the Furniture History Society
Goodison	Sir Nicholas Goodison, *Ormolu: The work of Matthew Boulton* (1974)
Harris, Bellaigue, Millar	John Harris, Geoffrey de Bellaigue, Oliver Millar, *Buckingham Palace* (1968)
Haskell & Penny	Francis Haskell & Nicholas Penny, *Taste and the Antique . . .* (1981)
Jagger	Cedric Jagger, *Royal Clocks – The British Monarchy and its Timekeepers 1300–1900* (1983)
Laking	Guy Francis Laking, *The Armoury of Windsor Castle . . .* (1904)
Levey	Sir Michael Levey, *The Later Italian Pictures in the Collection of H.M. The Queen* (1964)
Millar	Sir Oliver Millar, *The Tudor, Stuart and Early Georgian Pictures* (1963) and *The Later Georgian Pictures in the Collection of H.M. The Queen* (1969)
PRO	Public Record Office, London
QG, 1966	The Queen's Gallery, *George IV and the Arts of France* (1966)
QG, 1968	The Queen's Gallery, *Van Dyck Wenceslaus Hollar & The Miniature-Painters at the Court of the early Stuarts* (1968)
QG, 1974–5	The Queen's Gallery, *George III, Collector & Patron* (1974–75)
QG, 1978–9	The Queen's Gallery, *Holbein and the Court of Henry VIII* (1978–79)
QG, 1980–1	The Queen's Gallery, *Canaletto Paintings & Drawings* (1980–81)
RA	Royal Archives, Windsor Castle
Shearman	John Shearman, *The Early Italian Pictures in the Collection of H.M. The Queen* (1983)

Souchal I, II, and III   François Souchal, *French Sculptors of the 17th and 18th centuries. The reign of Louis XIV*. I A–F (1977), II G–L (1981), III M–Z (1987)

Strong, *Tudor Court*   Sir R. Strong and V.J. Murrell, *Artists of the Tudor Court*, Victoria and Albert Museum (1983)

Strong, 1983   Sir R. Strong, *The English Renaissance Miniature* (1983)

V&A, *Rococo*   Victoria & Albert Museum, *Rococo Art and Design in Hogarth's England* (1984)

White   Christopher White, *The Dutch Pictures in the Collection of H.M. The Queen* (1982)

Bibliographical Note

Many of the pictures in this exhibition have been discussed in detail in the volumes, by Lorne Campbell, Michael Levey, Oliver Millar, John Shearman and Christopher White, in the *Catalogue Raisonné* of The Queen's pictures. Bibliographical notes on them have therefore been limited to reference to these volumes, where full bibliographies will be found, and to the more important publications which have appeared since they were published. For pictures which have not yet been catalogued in detail, i.e., those of the French, later Flemish and German schools, bibliographical references are inevitably slightly fuller. The provenance of pictures is, in most instances, presented in summary form. In entries for the miniatures in the exhibition, bibliographical references have been restricted to the most recent publications; we are grateful to Mr Graham Reynolds for allowing us to draw on material assembled for his forthcoming catalogue of the earlier miniatures in The Queen's collection and to Mr A.V.B. Norman for writing the entries for Nos.127–31 below.

It should be pointed out that it is not possible, especially in a catalogue of this nature, to describe precisely the media in which certain paintings were executed. Research being carried out in the Scientific Department of the National Gallery, to which we would wish to record our continuing gratitude, is providing a growing body of analytical evidence for the use by artists of mixed media, even at a comparatively late date. In the ensuing entries the (presumed) predominant medium is listed.

I

Pictures

Hans Holbein the Younger (1497/8–1543)

1 Sir Henry Guildford (d.1532)

Oil on panel: 32½ × 26⅛ in., 82.6 × 66.4 cm. Inscribed: *Anno D: MCCCCCXXVII/Etatis.Suæ .xl ix:* on a *cartellino* painted over one of the type painted on pictures in the collection of John, 1st Lord Lumley (d.1609). In his inventory the portrait appears as 'drawne by Hance Holbyn'; later in the inventory the companion portrait of Lady Guildford, now in the City Art Museum, St Louis, is listed. The two portraits passed by descent to Lumley's great-nephew, the Earl of Arundel, who assembled the finest collection ever made of the work of Holbein. The portrait of Sir Henry belonged eventually to the Earl of Stafford and, probably soon after his death in January 1734, was acquired by the Crown, presumably at the wish of Queen Caroline.

A favourite of Henry VIII, Guildford held numerous posts in his service. He was Master of the Horse (1515–22) and Comptroller of the Household (the staff he holds may allude to the latter office) and was created a Knight of the Garter in 1526 (the collar of the Order is prominent in the portrait). As Comptroller, Guildford was responsible for authorizing payments for decorative work at Greenwich to Master Hans, who is assumed to have been Holbein. The portrait of Guildford is the only one to survive in England from his first period of activity in London, 1526–8. The preparatory drawing (at Windsor) for the portrait has the same grandeur of conception as the drawings, made at this time, of members of the family of Sir Thomas More. In laying out the painting with the drawing beside him Holbein lengthened appreciably the sitter's countenance. The finished portrait has a formidable authority, an almost terrifying detachment and a physical presence comparable to the portrait of More himself: very different in mood from the smaller and more introspective portraits of Holbein's later years in England. The condition of the portrait is very pure. Much gold paint is used in the costume and in the Garter collar and gold leaf in the cap-badge. The curtain and the climbing vine (?) in the background are features which had appeared in Holbein's slightly earlier work in Basel. The badge in Guildford's cap is etched with a pattern of objects which are the components of the *Typus Geometriae*, the iconographic formula used by Dürer in his *Melencolia I* of 1514 (Millar, No.28; QG, 1978–9, No.13; S. Foister, *Drawings by Holbein from the Royal Library Windsor Castle* (New York, 1983), pp.21–22, 33; J. Rowlands, *Holbein* (1985), p.133, No.25; J. Roberts, *Drawings by Holbein from the Court of Henry VIII*, Museum of Fine Arts, Houston (1987), No.9).

Jan Gossaert, called Mabuse (d.1532)

2 The Children of Christian II of Denmark

Oil on panel: 13$\frac{7}{16}$ × 18⅛ in., 34.2 × 46 cm. The children, brought to the Netherlands after their father had been driven out of Scandinavia in 1523: John (1518–32), Dorothea (1520–62) and Christina (1522–90). The sitters are apparently in mourning for their mother, Isabella of Austria, who had died on 19 January 1526 (Gossaert had been commissioned by Christian II to design her tomb); and when the King left the Netherlands in March 1526, the children remained in the care of their great-aunt, Margaret of Austria, at Malines, where Mabuse probably painted them. Princess Christina was, twelve years later, painted by Holbein in the famous full-length in the National Gallery which is connected with negotiations for a marriage between the Princess and Henry VIII.

Of the known versions of the composition, No.2 is unquestionably the finest; and recent cleaning revealed that it is in excellent condition. Some underdrawing is visible; the handling is extremely delicate and accomplished. There are *pentimenti* in the contours of the fruit, the hat of the boy and the cuffs and eyelids of the older girl.

It is extremely difficult, on the other hand, to establish the history of the picture. A version of the design in the collection of Henry VIII, recorded in the inventory of pictures at Whitehall in 1542, was almost certainly the picture hanging at Whitehall in the time of Charles I. There is no reference to such a portrait group in the Royal Collection, however, between the time of Charles I and the early eighteenth century. The children were by then, moreover, variously thought to be the children of Henry VII (on the back of No.2 is an inscription to this effect) or the children of Henry VIII. No.2 may, however, have

2

been bought at the sale of Charles I's goods by Gaspar Duarte; and the picture in the Duarte collection may, in turn, be the picture, recorded at Kensington early in the Georgian period, which could have been acquired by or for Queen Caroline, whose well-known enthusiasm for early historical portraits would certainly have been aroused by so entrancing a picture of, it was believed, the children of Henry VII (Campbell, No.34).

Raphael *(1483–1520)*

3 Portrait of the Artist

Oil(?) on panel: $16\frac{3}{4} \times 16\frac{5}{8}$ in., 42.7 × 42.2 cm. Inscribed on the left button on the doublet, in a circle: *RAFFAELLO.*; on the right, in the same way: *VRBINVS* [   ]. The missing section of the inscription was read by Passavant (1836) as: *FEC.*, but John Shearman (see below) considers this an unacceptable reading.

The picture has one of the most interesting histories of any in The Queen's collection. It illustrates two significant moments in the story of the cult of Raphael. The picture was presented to George III in 1781 by Lord

3

Cowper, who, in No.26, is surrounded by celebrated pictures by Raphael and contemplates a work by the painter which he may have been hoping to persuade the King to buy. By 1785 No.3 was hanging at Kensington where, in 1831, it was seen by Passavant who, in spite of its condition, was certain it was by Raphael. The Prince Consort, profoundly interested in Raphael's work, was probably encouraged by his reading of Passavant to endeavour to resurrect the portrait. Thomas Uwins, the Surveyor of Pictures, reported in February 1856 that he had found the picture. 'It is in the state in which it was at Kensington. I am afraid His Royal Highness will be shocked to see it. What ignorant repairer it can have been trusted to I am at loss to imagine! the grosness of the work

however makes it more easy to remove . . .' Later in the same year the picture was cleaned by Seguier. It was classified by Ruland as an autograph work in the Prince's *Raphael Collection*. The picture was consigned thereafter to almost a century of neglect and has only recently been re-established as a self-portrait painted at Urbino, *c*.1505–6. The portrait was cleaned in 1978. The panel has been cut on the left and right and at the bottom. Luisa Becherucci produced, in Shearman's words, 'a particularly sensitive assessment of its probable original format, with both hands and perhaps even a parapet'.

In support of the dating, Shearman compares the Netherlandish style in the painting of the landscape with the background in Raphael's *St George* (in Washington), probably painted in 1506; cites the stag as a quotation from Memling's *St John* (in Munich); and points out that the architecture in the landscape is typical of Raphael's work *c*.1506. As a portrait of Raphael, Shearman sets it convincingly between the youthful drawn self-portrait (*c*.1503) in the British Museum and the young man on the right in the *School of Athens* (1511). There are slight *pentimenti*: alterations to the right outline of the shirt, to the far side of the face and to the hair on that side, in the folds of the cap and the doublet, and to the tower of the church on the left (Shearman, No.217; C. Gould in *Apollo*, vol.CXIX (1984), pp.224–5; R. Jones and N. Penny, *Raphael* (1983), p.171).

Pieter Bruegel the Elder (d.1569)

4 The Massacre of the Innocents
COLOUR PLATE I (detail) facing page 16

Oil on panel: $43 \times 62\frac{1}{4}$ in., 109.2 × 158.1 cm. The edges of the panel have been cut at top and bottom and on the right; and of the signature (*BRVEGEL*) only the top of the letters is now visible, bottom right. The picture has a notable history. Probably the picture of the Massacre of the Innocents referred to by Van Mander; later it was in a group of pictures acquired by Charles II at Breda from William Frizell in 1660, when it was described as 'a Villadge wth souldiery Landskip & c^a of Olde Brughell, of his best manner'. It cost the King 1,000 florins. It had been in the collection of the Emperor Rudolph II in Prague. In 1648 a Swedish army removed most of the pictures from Prague to Sweden, where they became the property of Queen Christina who, in passing through the Netherlands on her way to Rome, left *en route* a number of her pictures, some of which were sold in 1656.

The remains of Bruegel's signature, the impeccable provenance and the quality of the painting combine to give it pride of place above all versions of the subject;[1] but before 1660, and possibly even before 1621, it had undergone a remarkable transformation when almost all the references to the Biblical story of the Massacre of the Innocents were suppressed. These can be seen in all their horror in, for instance, the version in Vienna, formerly considered to be the original but now attributed to Pieter Brueghel the Younger. Almost all the slaughtered babies

[1]The first scholar to recognize this in modern times was Lord Clark who informed the Lord Chamberlain in November 1941: 'I am confident that it is an original Brueghel and the finest in England'.

and those being hauled to their death were painted over with less disquieting objects: farm animals, poultry, bundles, crockery and the like. Flames (removed from the sky during a partial cleaning in 1941–2) were also added so that the picture could be described as the sacking of a village. The painting has suffered much damage during its long history, in addition to the re-interpretation of the Massacre. The main elements of the composition and the essential poignancy of the brushwork survive, however, to give full meaning to the horror of the scene. For historical and technical reasons it has been decided not to remove any of the earlier overpainting. As a result of previous treatments and the increased transparency of these repaints, indications of the children remain. They give an impression of the original impact of the painting. Some of the episodes in the Massacre had, in any case, not been painted over.

The figure in command of the group of knights in the centre of the composition, and the standard that floats above them, have also been painted over. The standard first displayed white crosses in allusion to the arms of Jerusalem and, by implication, to King Herod, who may have been shown originally as the leader of the knights. Beneath the overpaint on the tabard of the mounted herald on the right are traces of an imperial eagle, in reference to the Roman Empire under which Herod ruled. There are traces of a star on the inn-sign on the right which was perhaps at first too pointedly described as the 'Star Inn'. Lorne Campbell, in an exhaustive account of the picture (see below), lists, and analyses the status of, the other versions in which can still be seen what lies under the overpainting in No.4.

The armour and costume in No.4 have, as Campbell points out, 'a curiously archaic look'; but fashion in both armour and peasant dress would have survived long after their styles had become old-fashioned and the costumes should probably be regarded as 'contemporary dress'. This feature of the composition, combined with the marvellous depiction of a late afternoon on a peculiarly foul winter day – a mood Bruegel could evoke with an unsurpassed combination of verisimilitude and a kind of grim poetry – gives No.4 a specially vivid sense of misery. Campbell cites Terlinden's opinion (1942) that the subject was inspired 'partly by the execution of a sentence in a village where taxes had not been paid or where criminals were being harboured'. The leader of the company of knights would then be a bailiff or one of his representatives; the herald proclaims the legality of the

4

sentence which is being carried out; the mounted figures in red would be the bailiff's sergeants; the soldiers and knights represent units of the repressive forces of order employed by the Netherlandish authorities. Campbell dates No.4 *c.*1565–7 and points out that Bruegel began to paint snow landscapes 'during or immediately after the exceptionally severe winter of 1564–5'.

There are many passages in No.4 of very high quality and many demonstrations of Bruegel's free brushwork, subtle range of tone and texture, incisive handling of detail and uniquely melancholy temper in the heads. Much confident and nervous under-drawing is visible and a number of alterations were made in painting (Campbell, No.9).

Giovanni Bellini (*c.1430–1516*)

5 Portrait of a young Man

Oil(?) on panel: $17\frac{3}{8} \times 14$ in., 44×35.5 cm. Signed on the *cartellino*: *Joannes bellinus*. Consul Smith acquired, with other pictures from the Sagredo collection in Venice in 1752, 'Ritratto di Giò Bellino'. Among the pictures acquired by George III with the Smith collection in 1762, it appears as 'J Bellino: Portrait of himself with his name on board', the measurements given as $18 \times 14\frac{1}{2}$ in. (45.7×36.8 cm). John Shearman (see below) provides an amusing account of the history of the attribution of No.5 from the time of Crowe and Cavalcaselle. Georg Gronau in 1928 suggested that this outstandingly sensitive portrait was by Bellini and exposed 'the fallacy of the signature-test' which Morelli had established in the

5

mistaken belief that Bellini always signed in Roman capitals. Gronau suggested a date *c.*1505; Giles Robertson (*Giovanni Bellini* (1968), pp.110–11) compared the landscape background with the landscape in the altarpiece, signed and dated 1507, in S. Francesco della Vigna in Venice. Shearman also pointed out that the survival of the original *barbe* round all the edges of the panel suggests the removal of 'a once-integral frame'. He provides a good analysis of the state of the picture. The distant part of the landscape and the sitter's features are comparatively well preserved. There are *pentimenti* in the castle on the left, in the glance of the eyes and in the outlines of the hair. In the landscape there are traces of drawing with the wrong end of the brush and of palm-prints to consolidate the surface. In addition to making an instructive contrast with Raphael's *Self-portrait* (No.3) of the same period, No.5 is precisely the type of portrait by Bellini which Dürer would have seen in Venice (see No.40) (Shearman, No.37).

PLATE I
Detail from *The Massacre of the Innocents*
by Pieter Bruegel the Elder (No.4)

6

Cristofano Allori (1577–1621)

6 Judith with the Head of Holofernes

Oil on canvas: $47\frac{3}{8} \times 39\frac{1}{2}$ in., 120.4 × 100.3 cm. Inscribed: *Hoc Cristofori Allorii/Bronzinii opere natura/hactenus invicta pene/vincitur Anno 1613*. Cristofano used the adopted name, Bronzino, as his father, Alessandro, had done. Among the pictures acquired by Charles I with the Mantuan collection.

PLATE II
Detail from *An Allegory of Truth and Time*
by Annibale Carracci (No.10)

Cleaning and restoration (1978) and John Shearman's researches (see below) have established that No.6 is the earliest of a number of versions of 'Cristofano's most celebrated picture – indeed, the most celebrated of all Florentine Seicento pictures': more powerful in character and more finely painted, for instance, than the version in the Pitti Palace. There are considerable *pentimenti*: at many points in Judith's costume, in the servant's head and hands (holding the sack to receive the severed head) and in the cushion and the end of the bed. Shearman cites Baldinucci's account of the dramatic episode in the painter's life which is commemorated in the picture. Allori had a passionate love affair with a girl named La

Mazzafirra. After she had reduced him to misery he painted her as Judith; he himself allowed his beard to grow, and painted his self-portrait as Holofernes; and he painted the girl's mother as the old servant. The features of the heroine are more dramatically presented in this than in the other versions. Here she is described by Shearman as 'a credible portrait of the artist's persecutor', who is believed, incidentally, to have died in 1617. Shearman places No.6, which he evocatively describes as the work of an artist whose nerves were on edge, in a tradition most familiarly illustrated by Caravaggio's self-portrait as Goliath in the *David* in the Borghese Gallery and by Jacopo Ligozzi's *Judith* in the Pitti (Shearman, No.2: *Il Seicento Fiorentino*, Palazzo Strozzi, Florence (1986–7), pp.189–91; Claudio Pizzorusso's account of the version in the Pitti is vitiated by his dismissal of our No.6 as a copy).

Lorenzo Lotto (c.1480–1556)

7 Andrea Odoni (1488–1545)

Oil on canvas: $41 \times 45\frac{7}{8}$ in., 104.1 × 116.6 cm. Signed and dated: *Laurentius lotus/1527*. The portrait, painted when Lotto was living in Venice, was recorded in Odoni's house in the city by Marcantonio Michiel in 1532. A hundred years later it was in the collection of Lucas van Uffelen in Amsterdam; acquired by Gerard Reynst, it was among the pictures bought by the States of Holland, from the collection formed by him and his brother, for presentation to Charles II, in celebration of the Restoration, in 1660.

The sitter, whose father had moved from Milan to Venice in 1490, was a successful merchant and held minor offices in the Republic. He lived in a *palazzo* in Fondamenta del Gaffaro, which Vasari described as '*un allegro di virtuosi*'. Michiel (see above) describes Odoni in No.7 as contemplating antique marbles. Scholars have successively identified a number of the pieces. In the collector's hand is a *Diana* or *Artemis of the Ephesians*; a small statuette of *Hercules* is in the right background; the large marble head in the lower right corner is a version of the *Hadrian* busts; in the left background is a reduction of the *Hercules and Antaeus* now in the Palazzo Pitti; the female torso in the foreground may record a lost antique fragment or may be an invention by the painter; and beyond Odoni's left elbow are a *Hercules* (?) and a *Venus* or *Diana Washing*. The coat worn by Odoni is, it has been suggested, the old

Roman robe of thick black cloth, lined with wolf-skins, which appears in the inventory of 1555 of the effects of Odoni's brother. The above is a brief synopsis of the very detailed analysis of the composition in John Shearman's account (see below) in which there will also be found a summary of the different interpretations put upon the objects displayed by Lotto and his patron. Shearman suggests that Odoni is stating that 'although surrounded by objects which testify to his wealth, his culture, and especially his love of works of art, he uses them to declare that his first love is for Nature in a different sense, the Nature of gardens'; he emphasizes that No.7 is much more than a plain portrait of a collector; and he takes up the point, made by Anna Banti (1955), that No.7 is one of a group of portraits in which Lotto 'ostentatiously shared the urbanity of his sitters and showed himself extravagantly inventive in format, action and content'. These three aspects of the composition are combined, as they were so often by Lotto, in compositions of a profoundly individual temper, and they are reflected in such later portraits as Titian's *Jacopo Strada* in Vienna, Van Dyck's portrait of Lucas van Uffelen (a previous owner of No.7) in the Metropolitan Museum in New York and, it may be suggested, in such a composition as No.13 by Rembrandt who would almost certainly have known the portrait of Odoni when it was in Van Uffelen's possession.

There is an important *pentimento*, where the edge of the table cloth, lower right, was at first painted lower and nearer the surface of the picture. The large antique head was then painted over it, the edge of the table raised and drawn back, as it were, and the cloth pushed up by the head (Shearman, No.143; P. Zampetti in *The Genius of Venice 1500–1600*, Royal Academy (1983), No.46).

7

8

Bernardo Strozzi (1581–1644)

8 A Concert

Oil on canvas: $40 \times 48\frac{7}{8}$ in., 101.6×124.1 cm. Purchased by George III with the collection of Consul Smith, who had probably bought it in 1752 from the Sagredo family. It has been pointed out (see H. Potterton, below) that the old man and his young companion are, perhaps at the direction of a third person, actually tuning their instruments: a theorbo-lute and violin respectively. A tenor shawm is prominently shown resting on a volume (presumably of music) on the left. Some significance may be attached to the very different ages of the two musicians.

Generally regarded as the finest of very many versions of the composition and as the one to show most notably 'Strozzi's highly distinctive technique, with excessively rich impasto'. A date after the painter had left Genoa and, by 1631, was established in Venice, is generally accepted. Many obvious precedents in earlier Venetian painting could be found for Strozzi's subject-matter and, in particular, for the picturesque costume of the older figure (Levey, No.656; L. Mortari, *Bernardo Strozzi* (Rome, 1966), p.137; H. Potterton, *Venetian Seventeenth Century Painting*, National Gallery (1979), No.23).

Sir Anthony van Dyck (1599–1641)

**9 Thomas Killigrew (1612–83)
and (?) William, Lord Crofts (c.1611–77)**
COLOUR PLATE IV (detail) between pages 32 and 33

9

Oil on canvas: $52\frac{1}{4} \times 56\frac{1}{2}$ in., 132.7 × 143.5 cm. Signed and dated: *A van, Dyck, 1638.* Purchased by Frederick, Prince of Wales, in 1748 from George Bagnall who had married the widow of Sir Daniel Arthur, a Jacobite exile who is stated to have brought the picture, with others, from Spain. The Prince of Wales hung it over a fireplace in Leicester House.

Thomas Killigrew, seated in an attitude associated traditionally with Melancholy, was a courtier – he was Page of Honour to the King – dramatist, royalist and wit. After the Restoration he was Groom of the Bedchamber and Master of the Revels. He was granted a patent in 1662 to build and manage the Theatre Royal, Drury Lane. The identity of his companion had long been lost, but he can perhaps be identified as Killigrew's brother-in-law William, Lord Crofts, Master of the Horse to the Duke of York, Captain of the Queen's Guards and, later, a Gentleman of the Bedchamber to Charles II.

To acquire such a beautiful picture was characteristic of a Prince who had a feeling for the sheer quality of paint, and an enthusiasm for Dutch and Flemish painting of the seventeenth century, which link him, in matters of taste, with his grandson, the Prince Regent. There is no more superb example in The Queen's collection of Van Dyck's nervous handling, sense of pattern or refinement of mood. The picture sets, indeed, a formidable standard by which to assess other works in the *œuvre.* The debt to Titian, constantly felt in Van Dyck's English portraits, is clear in the restrained colour and in such passages as the warm-toned head silhouetted against the sky and recalling the head on the left of Titian's *Vendramin Family* in the National Gallery which was then in Van Dyck's possession. The Prince of Wales may not, on the other hand, have been aware of the poignancy of the composition. Killigrew's wife, Cecilia Crofts, had died at the beginning of the year in which the group was painted. He wears a ring on a black velvet band round his left wrist; and the small cross attached to his sleeve is decorated with the intertwined initials: CC. On the sheet of paper in his hand are drawings of two female statues, one perhaps intended for his wife, with her infant son at her side, the other perhaps for her sister Anne, who had died a fortnight later. The broken column should perhaps be read as an emblem of fortitude. The plain, but very rich, black costume worn by both sitters is seen in many of Van Dyck's finest portraits. The pattern, especially the detail of the figure on the right in profile with a paper in his left hand, may derive partly from the double portrait by Sebastiano del Piombo (formerly in Berlin) of Verdelotti and Ubretto (Millar, No.156; QG, 1968, No.14; C. Brown, *Van Dyck* (1982), p.212).

10

Annibale Carracci (1560–1609)

10 An Allegory of Truth and Time
COLOUR PLATE II (detail) facing page 17

Oil on canvas: 51 × 66⅝ in., 129.5 × 169.2 cm. It is not known when No.10 entered the collection. It is first certainly recorded in 1876, hanging at Buckingham Palace, but it is perhaps an unlikely purchase to have been made in the nineteenth century. The subject is almost certainly an allegory of the Triumph of Truth: Fortune, a winged figure, stands on the left and Bonus Eventus on the right, pouring a libation and holding in his left hand poppies and ears of corn. Behind, Time has drawn Truth up from a well into the light of day; and Truth tramples on a female figure, possibly intended to represent Deceit or Calumny.

Generally dated c.1584–5, on the grounds of strong stylistic resemblances (notably in type, in the construction of the figures and their placing within the overall design, and in the treatment of landscape) with Annibale's *Baptism* of 1585 in S. Gregorio, Bologna, and with the frescoes by Annibale, especially the frieze with the history of Jason, in the Palazzo Fava: resemblances even closer since the recent cleaning of the *Allegory* has revealed Annibale's fresh touch, rich play of shadow and vivid range of colour. The most obvious indications of changes during painting are in the left hand of the figure on the left and the drapery below it; in the foliage, perhaps originally extensive, in the upper left background; in the right arm of the prostrate figure; and in

the right leg and left arm of the figure on the right. Stylistically the picture is evidence of the influence of Correggio and Barocci.

A drawing of the *Judgement of Paris* in the Fogg Art Museum (1932.333), formerly attributed to Jan Liss but now usually attributed to Annibale and dated 1584, shows close similarities in composition, type, handling and colour with the *Allegory*. It has even been suggested that 'a lost or unexecuted painting of the *Judgement of Paris* was meant as a pendant to the *Allegory of Truth and Time*' (Levey, No.433; D. Posner, *Annibale Carracci* (1971), vol.I, p.29, vol.II, pp.10–11; A.W.A. Boschloo, *Annibale Carracci in Bologna* (The Hague, 1974), vol.I, pp.71, 72, vol.II, pp.176, 191; S.J. Freedberg, *Circa 1600* (1983), pp.14–16; D. DeGrazia, *Correggio and His Legacy*, National Gallery of Art, Washington (1984), No.124; C. Dempsey in *The Age of Correggio and the Carracci*, National Gallery of Art, Washington; Metropolitan Museum, New York; Pinacoteca Nazionale, Bologna (1986), p.249).

Sir Anthony van Dyck (1599–1641)

11 Charles I in three Positions

Oil on canvas: 33¼ × 39¼ in., 84.5 × 99.7 cm. Perhaps the most celebrated, undoubtedly the most searching, portrait by Van Dyck of the King whose service he had entered in 1632 and whose image he created almost single-handed for the benefit of posterity; but not acquired for the collection until 1822, when George IV bought it from William Wells of Redleaf for 1000 guineas. It had been commissioned for the use of Bernini who had been authorized by Pope Urban VIII to carve a marble bust of the King. Hopes were entertained in Rome that the King might lead England back into the Catholic fold; and friendly links between the Vatican and Whitehall were partly forged by the gift of pictures and works of art between the two courts. The commission to Bernini had apparently come from the Queen. The picture remained with the Bernini family in Rome until 1802, when it was secured on behalf of William Buchanan and Arthur Champernowne; it was subsequently in the collection of Walsh Porter whose son wrote on 21 December 1809 that the picture had been 'intended' for the Prince of Wales.

Van Dyck probably began work on the canvas in the second half of 1635. It was sent to Rome in the following spring. The finished bust was sent from Rome to London in April 1637, after it had been on public exhibition in

11

Rome. It was received with enthusiasm and encouraged the Queen to commission a companion bust of herself: a scheme that never came to fruition. The bust of the King was destroyed in the fire at Whitehall Palace in 1698.

The triple portrait may have been inspired by Lotto's portrait of a jeweller (now in Vienna, but then in the collection of Charles I); there is also an obvious parallel with De Champaigne's study (National Gallery) of Cardinal Richelieu; and Kneller's triple portrait of the Earl of Nottingham (National Portrait Gallery) would have assisted Rysbrack in the same way as No.11 had assisted Van Dyck.

Bernini in theory would not have needed anything more formal than three studies of the King's head as plainly presented as the studies of Lord Nottingham; nor was there any need to put them on one canvas. Van Dyck, perhaps immediately inspired by the King's Lotto, produced a masterpiece of painting, on which, incidentally, his reputation would rest in those artistic circles in Rome in which the picture was going to be seen. The sky sets off the three heads far more poetically than De Champaigne's or Kneller's plain tones; the colour scheme created by the three different costumes, the Garter ribbon and the one glimpse of the Garter star is exceptionally rich; and the faces are modelled with a subtlety and a refinement of touch seldom seen in Van Dyck's work at this stage of his career. The extreme care with which, to help the sculptor, the face is modelled in all three positions, must indicate that they were very largely painted *ad vivum*; but it is characteristic of Van Dyck's method, at a time when he was under pressure to produce portraits of the King, that he adapted the central head to at least one other pattern, a three-quarter-length in armour of which the finest version is at Arundel Castle. There was a tradition, recorded many years later by John Evelyn, that when Bernini first saw the triple portrait he was struck, not surprisingly, by 'something of funest and unhappy, which the Countenance of that Excellent Prince foreboded' (Millar, No.146, and *Van Dyck in England*, National Portrait Gallery (1982–3), No.22).

12

Jacopo Tintoretto (1518/19–94)

12 Girolamo Pozzo

Oil on canvas: 44 × 40 in., 111.8 × 93.9 cm. On the basis of the damaged inscription, *HIERONIMVS PVT . . .*, John Shearman (see below) identified the sitter as Girolamo di Giovanni Pozzo or da Pozzo, a goldsmith living in the parish of S. Geremia in Venice, and dated the portrait *c.*1550. It was in the collection of George III, but there are a number of references in inventories going back to the later Stuarts, even perhaps to the time of Charles I, with which it could possibly be linked. The earlier history of the portrait is all the more difficult to reconstruct because it was frequently attributed to Jacopo Bassano (Shearman, No.256).

13

Rembrandt van Rijn (1606–69)

**13 Jan Rijcksen (1561–1637) and his Wife, Griet:
'The Shipbuilder and his Wife'**
COLOUR PLATE V (detail) between pages 32 and 33

Oil on canvas: 45 × 66½ in., 114.3 × 168.6 cm. Signed and dated: *Rembrandt.f.:/1633.* The sitter was a prosperous shipbuilder who in 1631 was 'the highest-rated taxpayer on the Rapenburg in Amsterdam'. In 1585 he had married Griet Jansdochter, whose father was also a shipbuilder. Rembrandt's portrait of the couple was recorded in the inventory (7 November 1659) of the estate of their son Cornelis. In No.13 Rijcksen is interrupted by his wife who brings him a message while he is at his working table, his dividers in his right hand, his left on a sheet of paper on which he has drawn the keel, and sections through the hull, of a boat. One of the books lying on the table is open and on one of the leaves are drawings

of a similar character. A ruler (?) lies across the papers. The picture was later in the Gildemeester and Smeth van Alphen collections in Amsterdam (sold respectively in 1800 and 1810). It appeared at the Lafontaine sale at Christie's, 12 June 1811 (63), but was sold privately before the sale to the Prince Regent for 5,000 guineas. It was probably his most spectacular purchase. It arrived at Carlton House on 13 June 1811 and was hung in the Blue Velvet Room in time for the brilliant fête given by the Regent on 19 June in honour of the French royal family and the Duchess of York. In the Lafontaine sale catalogue No.13 had been described as 'The surprising Chef d'oeuvre of Rembrandt . . . known throughout Europe as the finest Performance in his second manner . . . a truly wonderful performance, far above all Praise . . .'

Painted two years after Rembrandt's move from Leiden to Amsterdam and one year later than the *Anatomy Lesson* which had established his reputation overnight as the most fashionable portrait painter in the city: at the beginning of the decade in which he painted more portraits on commission than at any other comparable period in his career. No.13 occupies 'a quite unique place in Amsterdam portraiture of the early 1630s': a superb example of Rembrandt's style and sense of composition at this period of his early maturity: strongly, but most subtly lit, very richly worked in texture, notably in the flesh and in the whites, and with a strong sense of 'a fleeting moment' in the daily life of the Rijcksens. The proportions of the composition, and the diagonal lines of the gestures, may indicate that Rembrandt had seen No.7. Of Rembrandt's four surviving double portraits, No.13 is the most dramatic, and the one in which the spatial relationships are most lucidly defined. The mood is very different, for instance, in the portrait, painted eight years later, of Cornelis Anslo in conversation with a young woman (H. Gerson, *Rembrandt Paintings* (1968), 234); but the impression of an actual moment, frozen in time, can be seen in other early commissioned portraits from the same date as No.13: *A Young man at a Desk* of 1631 (ibid., 54), for example, *A Young Man sharpening a Quill* (ibid., 111), or *Johannes Uyttenbogaert* of 1633 (ibid., 137). With his outstanding technical gifts and his power of characterization, Rembrandt engages the interest of sitter and spectator alike as no other Dutch painter had done hitherto. In certain pairs of single portraits Rembrandt creates the same dramatic and psychological link (across the boundaries of the frames, as it were) that bind the figures together in No.13 (see for example the pair of portraits in Vienna or the more fashionable pair (1633) divided between Cincinatti and New York, ibid., 140, 141; 153, 154). David Smith (see below) has written an account of the antecedents, and later influence, of No.13 and of its significance as an essay by Rembrandt in the 'emerging imagery of domesticity' and in capturing 'a fleeting and essentially unique moment of encounter'. He cites Cats's treatise on marriage with its emphasis on the partnership in a true marriage between the man's brains and the woman's industry and stout leadership (White, No.160; D.R. Smith, 'Rembrandt's Early Double Portraits and the Dutch Conversation Piece', *Art Bulletin*, vol.LXIV (New York, 1982), pp.259–88; and see particularly the very detailed account in *A Corpus of Rembrandt Paintings*, by various authors, Stichting Foundation Rembrandt Research Project, vol.II (Amsterdam, 1986), pp.367–77, A77, with, incidentally, a discussion on the possible loss of $c.6\frac{3}{4}$ in., 17.1 cm, from the top of the canvas).

Domenico Fetti (c.1588/9–1623)

14 Vincenzo Avogadro

Oil on canvas: $45\frac{1}{8} \times 35\frac{1}{2}$ in., 114.6 × 90.2 cm. Inscribed: *VINC^S AVOG^S REC.ECCL.S.S.GER.ET/PROT. MANT. ANNO N. DCX[ ]/ÆTA. SVE ANN XXXV.* The sitter was rector of the church of SS. Gervaso e Protaso in Mantua. He clasps a small book, probably a prayer-book, in his hand as he stands by a table on which is a crucifix. The damaged part of the inscription probably contained an extra digit. Fetti painted for Avogadro's church in 1619–20 an altarpiece, *St Martin in Ecstasy*, and it is likely that his portrait was painted at the same time. Fetti had begun to work at the Mantuan court in 1613. He would have seen in Mantua the celebrated collections which were so soon to be dispersed; and a number of his own works were to be among those acquired by Charles I.

The portrait of Avogadro was in the collection of Consul Smith, but at the time of the purchase of his collection by George III, and for some time afterwards, was attributed to Van Dyck. Not until 1946 was the portrait, with its rich, almost tangible atmosphere, assured and nervous handling, and keen grasp of a sitter's personality, recognized (by the late Colin Agnew) as a fine work by Fetti (Levey, No.470; H. Potterton, *Venetian Seventeenth Century Painting*, National Gallery (1979), No.8).

Rembrandt van Rijn (1606–69)

15 Agatha Bas (1611–58): 'The Lady with a Fan'

Oil on canvas: $41\frac{1}{2} \times 33$ in., 105.2 × 83.9 cm. Signed and dated: *Rembrandt f./1641*, and inscribed: *Æ 29*. The companion portrait of Nicolaas van Bambeeck, to whom Agatha Bas had been married in 1638, is in the Musée Royal des Beaux-Arts in Brussels. He was a merchant and a neighbour of Rembrandt in Amsterdam, and was later in the group, with Rembrandt, which put up money for Hendrick Uylenburgh's art-dealing business. The two portraits were imported into England from Holland by Nieuwenhuys in 1814 and sold at Christie's, 29 June 1814 (76, 77). No.15 was sold later by Smith to Lord Charles Townshend and from his sale, 4 June 1819 (32), was bought by Lord Yarmouth for George IV.

In both portraits Rembrandt places the sitter, as a form of support, behind an arched opening. The wife's left hand rests on the upright of this opening and her fan falls outside the ledge at the bottom; her husband leans with

14

15

his right arm on the ledge and places his left hand on it. The two portraits are, therefore, designed as a pair, but there is not the dramatic involvement between husband and wife that there is in the pairs of portraits mentioned in association with No.13 (see Gerson, op. cit., 232, 233). In the eight years that separate the two works Rembrandt's rendering of light has become subtler; the sitters are placed between full light and full shadow; and there is a new reserve, in harmony, in this instance, with the introspective glance of his sitter and with 'the stylistic impulses of his time'. It is perhaps the most sophisticated of the fashionable portraits which Rembrandt painted in the 1640s. The main compositional device used in No.15 is partly anticipated in such portraits as the more outspoken portrait of Maria Trip (1639) in the Rijksmuseum (ibid., 194); and is used to much the same effect as in No.15 in the portrait of a girl (1641) formerly in the Lanckoronski collection (ibid., 224); it recurs much later, and in a much more relaxed mood, in the painting, in Berlin, of Hendrickje at an open door (ibid., 339) (White, No.162).

Frans Hals (c.1580–1666)

16 Portrait of a Man

Oil on canvas: $45\frac{3}{4} \times 35\frac{1}{2}$ in., 116.1 × 90.1 cm. Inscribed: *ÆTAT SVÆ 36/AN. 1630*. There are possible traces of a signature. Recorded at Buckingham House in the time of George III, but possibly acquired by Frederick, Prince of Wales.

Painted at the beginning of the decade in which Hals achieved his greatest popularity as a portrait painter. It was also, as Slive has pointed out, the decade in which Rembrandt (see No.13) painted more portraits than at any other time in his career (*Frans Hals*, vol.I (1970), p.112). Hals's portraits of the 1630s illustrate a change in style towards a simple, more monumental presentation. No.16 should be compared, for instance, with the portrait of Paulus van Beresteyn, with its angular design and slightly neurotic glance, painted ten years earlier (ibid., vol.II (1970), pl.27). The comparison also illustrates the change in fashion that has taken place: the move towards

27

16

plain black from the gaily coloured and richly embroidered costumes of the previous decades. No.16 has the ruddy fleshtones and the fine clean blacks of the *Banquet of the St George Civic Guard Company*, which Hals had completed a few years earlier. There are traces of substantial alterations to the silhouette of the figure (White, No.56).

Johannes Vermeer (1632–75)

17 A Lady with a Gentleman at the Virginals

Oil on canvas: $28\frac{7}{8} \times 25\frac{3}{8}$ in., 73.3×64.5 cm. Signed: *IVMeer* (initials in monogram). On the lid of the instrument, which is very similar to documented instruments by the elder Andries Ruckers, is painted the text: *MVSICA LETITIÆ CO[ME]S[MEDECINA DOLOR[IS]*; the reading of the letters concealed by the lady's head and shoulders is inevitably conjectural. On the tiled floor lies a bass viol.

Recorded in a sale in Amsterdam, 16 May 1696 (6); subsequently in the collection of Giovanni Antonio Pellegrini who had probably acquired it when he was working in The Hague in 1718; sold by his widow to Consul Smith, with whose collection it was acquired by George III. At that time the picture was attributed to Frans van Mieris; later it was ascribed by Mrs Jameson and Waagen to Eglon van der Neer. Redgrave (note on the relevant sheet of his inventory) was thoroughly confused by the artist's signature which he first recorded as 'Jan Van der meer'.

Christopher White (see below) gives a good account of the virginals and the decoration thereon; and suggests that the other 'props' belonged to the painter. The painting hanging on the wall, of which only part is seen, represents the Roman Charity and is clearly the work of a northern Caravaggist, again possibly at that time in Vermeer's possession. The subject of the painting and the message painted on the lid may both allude to the pleasures and sorrows of love. As White points out: 'The association between music and love was common in Holland in the seventeenth century and can be read at various levels'. It would be idle, however, to attempt to define precisely the relationship between the two figures. The lack of overt action and the notable understatement of emotion are quintessential aspects of Vermeer's late style. Reflected in the mirror above the instrument are the woman's head and the legs of the painter's easel.

No.17 is normally dated, with the *Concert* in the Isabella Stewart Gardner Museum in Boston, *c*.1665. Gowing (1952) considered it to be one of the paintings by Vermeer (from the middle period) which 'introduce that studied obliquity of theme, with its delicate symbolic accompaniment, which provides the matter for his later works'. To Rosenberg and Slive (1966), however, the emphasis on perspective and the dominance of the space over the figures suggested a late date, *c*.1670. The light is used to

17

18

great effect to enhance the recession into space and has a lucid intensity totally different from the atmospheric effect which it is used to achieve by De Hooch in, for instance, No.17. Blankert (see below) dates the picture 1664 and points to the balance between rest and movement, between mathematical order and 'sensibilité'; and describes the treatment of space as a De Hooch carried to perfection. Infra-red reflectography reveals that the man was at first placed closer to the girl (White, No.230; P.C. Sutton in *Masters of Seventeenth-Century Dutch Genre Painting*, Philadelphia Museum of Art; Gemäldegalerie, Berlin (West); Royal Academy (1984), No.119; G. Aillard, A. Blankert and J.M. Montias, *Vermeer* (Paris, 1986), pp.118–20, 185, No.16).

Aelbert Cuyp (1620–91)

18 The Passage Boat

Oil on canvas: $49 \times 56\frac{3}{4}$ in., 124.4×144.2 cm. Signed: *A. cüyp*. Acquired by George IV with the Baring collection in 1814. Cuyp's work, which had been little known outside Dordrecht until the end of the eighteenth century, became so popular in England in the Napoleonic period that, by about 1825, 'a near monopoly' of his pictures had been established here (see *Aelbert Cuyp in British Collections*, National Gallery (1973)); and George IV owned five other important pictures by Cuyp in addition to No.18.

Cuyp, who lived almost all his life at Dordrecht, painted a number of magnificent pictures of the traffic on the Merwede and the Maas: pictures notable above all for their rendering of the relation between water, sky and shipping against a low horizon, often in an evening of golden, autumnal, beauty. In No.18 the passage boat appears to be arriving at a landing-stage to the accompaniment of a drum. The Dutch flag flies at the masthead and the peak. It is probably the boat which plied daily between Dordrecht and Rotterdam. The vessels in the background may be an allusion to the visit of the Dutch fleet to Dordrecht in the summer of 1647; and on grounds of costume the picture can probably be dated *c.*1650. The particularly vigorous brushwork in the clouds would support the dating. Cuyp's painting of the vessels would have been based on material collected on sketching tours on the rivers of Holland (White, No.39).

Sir Peter Paul Rubens (1577–1640)

19 Milkmaids with Cattle in a Landscape: 'The Farm at Laeken'

Oil on panel: $33\frac{3}{4} \times 49\frac{9}{16}$ in., 85.7×125.9 cm. The panel was extended by Rubens, as was often his practice, as the composition developed. There is a strip added at the top (*c.*5 in., 12.7 cm), on the left (*c.*2$\frac{3}{4}$ in., 7 cm) and on the right (*c.*5$\frac{3}{4}$ in., 14.6 cm). Among the pictures by Rubens which had belonged to Arnold Lunden, husband of Rubens's sister-in-law Susanna Fourment. Lunden's collection also contained the portrait of a woman in the National Gallery (the so-called '*Chapeau de Paille*') and the female portrait at Windsor. In the eighteenth century there was a tradition that Rubens had painted the picture to prove to Wildens that he was as good at painting landscapes as figures. When the Lunden collection was eventually dispersed, No.19 was sold to L.J. Nieuwenhuys for 30,000 francs on 8 November 1817. In due course, when it was in the Aynard collection, it was submitted to the Prince Regent. It was eventually delivered at Carlton House on 7 July 1821.

Probably painted *c.*1617–18 and usually associated stylistically, and in the use of a number of elements in the design, with two other landscapes of this type by Rubens: *Polder Landscape with Cows* in Munich and the *Landscape with Cows and Sportsmen* at Dahlem (Adler (see below), Nos.27 and 31); a drawing of an ox in the Albertina (8.253) was probably used in connection with No.19. The shepherdess in Rubens's *Adoration of the Shepherds* in Marseilles, part of an altarpiece commissioned on 27 December 1616, is fairly close to the central female figure in No.19. A preparatory drawing for the kneeling milkmaid is in the Albertina (8.294). The church in the distance of No.19 is almost certainly Nôtre-Dame at Laeken. Only the choir survived the demolitions of 1894.

X-ray shows that the grain of the panel used for the addition on the left runs vertically, in conflict with the horizontal grain of the main panel; and it appears that the composition had been taken some way, but not very far, on the main panel before Rubens decided to enlarge it. In the development of Rubens's landscapes, No.19 is the first in which he painted a tranquil sunlit scene of Flemish country life against a gently undulating landscape and a peaceful distance, with none of the dramatic action or geological contortions which characterize his earlier landscapes. With its rich colour, fresh touch and luminous atmosphere, as well as the painter's affectionate

19

painting of animals, country people and still-life, it is not surprising that Louis XV, when he saw them in 1746, should have wanted to acquire M. Lunden's '*Chapeau de Paille*' and '*Farm at Laeken*' (according to a tradition recorded by Nieuwenhuys (*A Review of the Lives and Works of some of the most eminent Painters* (1834), p.204));

or that George IV should have considered No.19 to be one of the pictures which his collection at Carlton House in 1821 'actually wanted' (W. Adler, *Landscapes, Corpus Rubenianum Ludwig Burchard*, part XVIII, I (1982), No.20, with useful bibliography).

PLATE III
Detail from *The Card-players*
by Pieter de Hooch (No.23)

The following pages:

PLATE IV
Detail from *Thomas Killigrew and (?) William, Lord Crofts*
by Sir Anthony van Dyck (No.9)

PLATE V
Detail from *Jan Rijcksen and his Wife, Griet*
by Rembrandt van Rijn (No.13)

20

Sir Anthony van Dyck (1599–1641)

20 The Mystic Marriage of St Catherine

Oil on canvas: 49¾ × 47 in., 126.4 × 119.4 cm. Signed: *A VAN DYCK*. Purchased by George IV, probably in 1821, and subsequently placed in the Blue Drawing-Room at Carlton House. Formerly in Brussels in the possession of the de Bustancy family, from whom it was acquired in 1802 by the Chevalier de Burtin, who imported it into England.

Painted *c.*1630: a distinguished and characteristic example of Van Dyck's Counter-Reformation style in the years between his return to Antwerp from Italy in 1627 and his departure for London in the spring of 1632: still solid in form, but refined in colour and execution; restrained and well-bred in feeling; fundamentally Venetian in type and in its range of tones; and, on this scale, eminently suitable for display in the private chapel of a royal or aristocratic patron. Charles I and Henrietta Maria in fact received as a New Year's gift from Sir Balthazar Gerbier in December 1631 'an exceedingly beautiful Our Lady and St Catherine made by the hand of van Dyck' which had been placed by the Archduchess Isabella in the private chapel used by Queen Marie de' Medici in Brussels. The 'types' of the Infant Christ and the Saint recur in a number of pictures by Van Dyck (Millar, No.162; QG, 1968, No.13).

PLATE VI
Detail from *Coast Scene with the Rape of Europa*
by Claude Gellée, called 'Le Lorrain' (No.21)

33

Claude Gellée, called 'Le Lorrain' (1600–82)

21 Coast Scene with the Rape of Europa
COLOUR PLATE VI (detail) facing page 33

Oil on canvas: 53 × 40 in., 134.6 × 101.6 cm. The original painted surface is 51¾ × 38¾ in., 131.4 × 98.4 cm. Signed and dated: *CLAVDE GILLE IVRI/ROMÆ 1667*. Bought for George IV for £2,100 at Lord Gwydir's sale, Christie's, 9 May 1829 (81). Formerly in the collection of the marquise de Bandeville (sold in Paris, 1787), granddaughter of Philippe de Graveron for whom (see below) the picture may have been painted.

Michael Kitson has written that only with Claude was 'the mood as well as the iconography of pastoral poetry . . . fully mastered by a great painter', and, stressing the painter's devotion to Ovid's *Metamorphoses* as a source for his mythological landscapes: 'Here was a world both ordered and varied, at once simplified, as the elements of a pastoral poem are simplified, and full of incident for the eye to dwell upon; a world designed for the imagination to enter and wander about in'. The story of the rape of Europa occurs in the second book of the *Metamorphoses*. Jupiter, enamoured with Europa, assumed the shape of a bull with a snow-white hide and mingled with the herd while Europa, daughter of Agenor, and her companions were gathering flowers by the sea. Encouraged by his apparent gentleness she hung garlands on his horns and mounted on his back, whereupon he swam off into the sea with her. Claude's bull is very closely modelled on Ovid's text in which special attention is paid to the deep folds of skin hanging along his flanks and to his small, beautifully formed, horns.

The story was illustrated by Claude, always in the same idyllic terms, on a number of occasions between 1634 and 1670. In the earlier year he painted a large canvas of the subject (now in the Kimbell Art Museum) which, in the same year, he reproduced in an etching and in which all the elements of the story, as set out more spaciously in No.21, are present. In 1647 Claude painted the variant, now in Utrecht, which he recorded in his *Liber Veritatis* (No.111; see ed. by M. Kitson (1978), pp.120–1) and which is close in composition to No.21. In 1655 he painted for Pope Alexander VII the variant, now in the Pushkin Museum, Moscow, recorded in the *Liber* (No.136; ibid., pp.136–7). No.21 is a variant, painted probably from the drawing in the *Liber* and not from the

Pope's picture. On the verso of the sheet in the *Liber* is inscribed, probably in another hand, the name of Philippe de Graveron which refers to this second version of the composition and which may have been written on the sheet when the repetition was ordered from Claude in 1667. Röthlisberger has pointed out that there would have been a 'certain *cachet*' attached to a composition painted for the Pope; but in the second treatment of the subject a 'pervasive transformation' (in Kitson's phrase) has taken place. A smaller version, with more marked variations in detail and composition, had been painted by Claude in 1658 (*Liber*, No.144; ibid., pp.141–2). Claude also produced four finished drawings of the subject.

No.21, always recognized as one of the most sublimely poetic of all Claude's late works, is therefore also the culminating variation on one of the painter's favourite themes. To the qualities defined so sensitively by Kitson (the softened colours and atmosphere; 'the serene, spacious and almost ethereal landscape, in which the forms are so insubstantial that they hardly seem to interrupt the continuity of the air') must be added the qualities of colour and touch which recent cleaning has revealed. The composition was very carefully worked, and worked over, by the painter at all points, notably, for instance, in the foreground. He also shifted many of the elements in the design, such as the figures and the cattle, as the composition was developed. The execution throughout is remarkably refined, and even in such tiny details as the flowers a great variety of colour was used (M. Röthlisberger, *Claude Lorrain: the Paintings* (New Haven, 1961), vol.I, pp.325–9; M. Kitson, *The Art of Claude Lorrain*, Hayward Gallery, London (1969), No.36, and 'Claude's earliest "Coast Scene with the Rape of Europa"', *Burl. Mag.*, vol.CXV (1973), pp.775–9; *Claude Gellée dit Le Lorrain*, National Gallery of Art, Washington, and Grand Palais, Paris (1982–3), p.208, No.48 bis; see also No.15 and pp.331–4; for an analysis of the structure of the paint, see K. Groen in *The Bulletin of the Hamilton Kerr Institute*, No.1 (1988), pp.48–65).

21

22

Sir Peter Paul Rubens (1577–1640)

22 The Assumption of the Virgin

Oil on panel: $40\frac{3}{16} \times 26$ in., 101.9×66 cm. Purchased by Lord Yarmouth for the Prince Regent at the sale of Henry Hope's pictures, Christie's, 29 June 1816 (79), and placed in the Bow-Room on the ground floor at Carlton House. Formerly in the collections of A. Bout in The Hague (sold 1733) and the comte d'Orsay in Paris (sold 1790); secured in Paris by Christie, bought from him by John Purling and sold from his collection in London in 1801. Subsequently in the Sir Simon Clarke and George Hibbert sale, Christie's, 15 May 1802 (56).

The Assumption provided an outstandingly important theme in the glorification of the Virgin at the time of the Counter-Reformation and was particularly popular in many forms and on every scale during the revival of Catholicism in the Southern Netherlands: a movement in which Rubens was deeply involved. The subject occupied him at regular intervals between his return to Antwerp in the autumn of 1608 and the mid-1630s. David Freedberg (see below) has provided a most valuable analysis of the popularity of the subject and of the literary and artistic sources available to Rubens. The main elements of the story are to be found in the *Golden Legend* (for English readers, one of the original accounts, the Latin text of the Pseudo-Melito, is conveniently printed in M.R. James, *The Apocryphal New Testament* (1924), pp.209–18); a principal popular contemporary source was Jerome Nadel's *Adnotationes et Meditationes in Evangelia* (Antwerp, 1595 and 1607). Rubens's distinctive contribution to the visual treatment of the subject is the inclusion of the holy women among the Apostles. His handling of the subject was influenced by such painters as the Carracci, Barocci and Guido Reni; but the main source was Titian's great picture in the Frari in Venice.

In No.22 the upper half of the composition is very closely linked with the upper part of the altarpiece of the Assumption now in the Kunsthistorisches Museum, Vienna (Freedberg, No.37). The lower part of the altarpiece is no less closely associated with a *modello* in The Hermitage (ibid., No.46). It would obviously be convenient if the two *modelli* could be identified with the '*duo modella continentia historiam Assumptionis B. Mariae Virginis, diverso modo depicta*' which Rubens, already described in Antwerp as 'the god of painters', submitted to the Chapter of Antwerp Cathedral on 22 April 1611 and on the strength of which he secured the commission to paint an Assumption for the high altar. The altarpiece now in Vienna was in fact set up in the Mary Chapel in the Jesuit Church in Antwerp. Objection to the hypothesis that Rubens composed the altarpiece on the basis of No.22 and the *modello* in The Hermitage is founded on the belief (expressed principally by Baudouin and Held) that No.22 is, in style, later than the *modello* in Leningrad. This is an understandable point of view, but there are passages in No.22, notably the two holy women and the drapery they hold, which are possibly not inconsistent with a date *c*.1611: perhaps also acceptable in the light of the formal qualities in the sketch. In the upper part of No.22 it is clear that after some indecision Rubens gave to the design a round-headed form which coincides almost exactly with the outline of the top of the Vienna altarpiece and controls the placing of the cherubs who surround the Virgin. There are in the *modello* a number of significant *pentimenti*. The kneeling figure in the foreground was first placed more in profile to the spectator; his original right hand is clearly seen under the tomb slab. The cloud of cherubs supporting the Virgin are based in part on Rubens's study of Pordenone's fresco in S. Niccolò in Treviso. The lower part of the *modello* contains elements used again by Rubens in the slightly later *Assumption*, now in Brussels (Freedberg, No.38), painted for the church of the Discalced Carmelites in Brussels. In particular, in No.22 we see the evolution of the kneeling foreground figure towards his equivalent in the Brussels altarpiece. No.22 was engraved *c*.1650 by Schelte a Bolswert. To the copies listed by Freedberg should be added a good early copy on panel, in a Belgian private collection, with slight, but important, differences, indicating that it may have been painted before No.22 reached its present state (F. Baudouin, 'Altars and Altarpieces before 1620', *Rubens before 1620* (Princeton, 1972), pp.45–91; and *Rubens et son Siècle* (Antwerp, 1972), pp.45–73; W. Prohaska, *Peter Paul Rubens*, Kunsthistorisches Museum, Vienna (1977), No.16; W. Koshatzky, *Die Rubens Zeichnungen in der Albertina* (Vienna, 1977), under No.8; J.S. Held, *The Oil Sketches of Peter Paul Rubens* (Princeton, 1980), vol.I, No.375; D. Freedberg, *Rubens The Life of Christ after the Passion*, *Corpus Rubenianum Ludwig Burchard*, part VII (1984), No.35; C. White, *Peter Paul Rubens* (1987), p.106).

23

Pieter de Hooch (1629–84)

23 The Card-players

COLOUR PLATE III (detail) facing page 32

Oil on canvas: $30 \times 26\frac{1}{8}$ in., 76.2×66.4 cm. A small amount of original painted canvas is turned over on the right. Signed and dated: *P.D.H./1658.* Acquired by George IV for £700 from Lord Farnborough on 27 April 1825. Formerly in the Walraven, Van der Lande and Van der Schley collections in Amsterdam (sold respectively in 1763, 1789 and 1818). On the remains of a seal on the stretcher is a cameo with a leopard (?) *courant.*

Nieuwenhuys, who owned the picture briefly in 1823, considered that 'for the management of its light and shadow, this is the most surprising picture I have seen of this painter . . . so striking for its masterly treatment, that its novelty awakened the attention of collectors both in France and England . . . but I can only observe that specimens of this kind are very rare' (op. cit., pp.155–6). Smith (1833) refers to the 'consummate knowledge of the principles of art' which the picture displays.

The picture is, in fact, a work of unrivalled beauty from that short period, *c.*1655–62, when De Hooch, living in Delft, produced a series of masterpieces. They illustrate, in Sutton's phrase (see below), the 'full flowering of the naturalistic impulse' in De Hooch's art, in which he creates an illusion of space primarily through a remarkably sophisticated rendering of light and shade so as to produce an almost tangible atmosphere. The mood is enhanced by the clearly defined space, subtly extended by opening a door or window into a space beyond; by the lack of dramatic gestures in the figures; and by very fine colour. In No.23 the atmosphere is created principally by the fall of light upon soft, often deeply shadowed, forms, especially on the hair, collar and thigh of the seated drinker on the left of the table. The card on the floor, near fragments of a pipe, is the five of hearts; on the table is the ten of hearts or diamonds; the woman holds a card of spades or clubs; and her companion perhaps holds his thumb over an ace. If these elements in the design were intended to evoke in the spectator allusions to love in various forms, their message is put across with extreme restraint. It should perhaps be pointed out that the male figures do not appear to be soldiers. The unhurried way in which the man on the left raises his glass to his lips epitomizes the restraint, indeed the whole magic, of this marvellous picture.

Cleaning has revealed a marked lightening of tone in the composition. It is easier now to discern the drawn lines with which De Hooch constructed his perspective. On the floor the separate stones are carefully painted, leaving the grey ground to serve as the dividing line between them. De Hooch's fresh, crisp touch is particularly noticeable in the lady's head and the man's right hand holding the card. There are slight alterations in painting in many of the elements in the composition; and a remarkable richness of colour and, above all, of light, is created by De Hooch's use of softened tones worked into the whites (White, No.85; see particularly the passages by Slive (1966) and Sutton (1980) to which he refers).

Guido Reni (1575–1642)

24 Cleopatra with the Asp

Oil on canvas: $44\frac{3}{4} \times 37\frac{3}{8}$ in., 113.7×94.9 cm. Acquired by Frederick, Prince of Wales. George Vertue saw it in 1749 in Leicester House, hanging in the Closet, in which the Prince had put the pictures he valued most highly; 'so beautifull strong clear & Natural. of the finest taste of that skillfullest artist'. It was subsequently hung by George III in a carefully arranged display of predominantly seicento pictures in the Closet at Buckingham House (see

24

F. Russell, 'King George III's picture hang at Buckingham House', *Burl. Mag.*, vol.CXXIX (1987), pp.524–31). The profound admiration of Guido at that time is well expressed in A.J. Dezallier d'Argenville, *Abrégé de la Vie des plus fameux Peintres* (Paris, 1762), vol.II, p.101: '*il possedoit l'idée du beau si parfaitement, qu'il le faisoit briller même dans un visage flétri & meurtri ... le Guide a établi toutes les richesses de la peinture*'.

Considered by Sir Michael Levey to be the earliest surviving treatment of the theme by Guido, from the late 1620s or very early 1630s. Confirmation now exists (see Pepper, below) for Sir Michael's suggestion that No.24 is the picture of this subject painted by Guido, at the request of Palma Giovane, for Boselli, a merchant in Venice, to form part of a series of pictures of which the others were by Palma himself, Renieri and Guercino. From Renieri's collection it was bought by Domenico Fontana (Levey, No.576; C.Garboli, *L'opera completa di Guido Reni* (Milan, 1971), No.122; D.S. Pepper, *Guido Reni* (1984), pp.266–7, No.136).

25

Giovanni Antonio Canal, called *Canaletto* (1697–1768)

25 A Regatta on the Grand Canal

Oil on canvas: $30\frac{3}{8} \times 49\frac{1}{2}$ in., 77.2×125.7 cm. The two paintings of Venetian festivals (see also No.28) are spectacular additions to the series of fourteen views (on a uniform scale, but smaller than these two scenes) of the Grand Canal which were engraved by Antonio Visentini and published in Venice by G.B. Pasquali in 1735. The two festive scenes were pls.XIII and XIV in the volume. The series was part of the unrivalled collection of paintings, drawings and prints by Canaletto which was one of the special glories of the collection formed by his particular friend Joseph Smith, British Consul in Venice, and acquired by George III in 1762. The set of views of the Grand Canal was hung by the King at one stage in the Gallery at Kew. When, with so many other works by Canaletto, they hung on the walls of Smith's villa on the mainland or small palace on the Grand Canal, they would have been a marvellous advertisement of the kind of

picture, or sets of pictures, which Smith would undertake to commission from the painter, variously described as whimsical, overworked, covetous and greedy. The series would have gained further publicity through Visentini's engravings.

The two pictures of festivals were almost certainly painted after the series had been completed. Such pairs of pictures, illustrating these occasions, were among the most popular products in Canaletto's workshop. In No.25 the coat of arms on the *macchina* in the left foreground, beside Palazzo Balbi, is that of Carlo Ruzzini, Doge from June 1732 to his death in January 1735. The annual regatta on the Grand Canal, held on the Feast of the Purification of the Virgin (2 February), was instituted in 1315, although regattas were also held to mark special occasions. The course was from the Motta di S. Antonio (the site of the present Giardini Pubblici), up to the post or *Zirada* erected off the Ponte della Croce, and back to the Volta di Canal, where a richly decorated pavilion, the *macchina della regatta*, had been erected and on which the winners received prizes of coloured flags. In No.25 the race is rowed by light gondolas manned by a single gondolier. Canaletto's treatment of the theme is closely related to Carlevaris's painting of the regatta held in 1709 in honour of Frederick VI, King of Denmark; and he never fundamentally altered the formula.

The banks of the Grand Canal are lined with spectators; windows and balconies have been decorated with hangings; many of the boats have been specially decked; and many spectators are in ceremonial dress. In accordance with his usual practice, Canaletto composed the scene from two viewpoints (the right bank has been opened out); and the distance (with the Rialto just discernible) has been diminished (Levey, No.396; QG, 1980–1, No.19; J.G. Links, *Canaletto* (1982), pp.73–74; A. Corboz, *Canaletto Una Venezia immaginaria* (Milan, 1985), vol.I, pp.206–7, vol.II, P.83).

Johan Zoffany (1733–1810)

26 The Tribuna of the Uffizi
FRONT AND BACK COVER (colour details)

Oil on canvas: $48\frac{5}{8} \times 61$ in., 123.5×154.9 cm. The Tribuna had been built in the Uffizi by Bernardo Buontalenti in 1585–9 as a shrine to contain a selection of the most famous, exotic and precious works of art in the Medici collections. Queen Charlotte, who had heard of Zoffany's plan to go to Italy in the summer of 1772, commissioned him to 'paint for Her, the Florence Gallery'. As a room, the Tribuna was in the tradition of the earlier *Wunder-kammern*; Zoffany's picture is a late essay in the tradition of painted views of crowded cabinets and galleries established by (in the main) Flemish painters of the seventeenth century, a genre of which Queen Charlotte owned a good example. In a number of pictures painted for the Queen the painter had demonstrated his remarkable ability to paint works of art in their setting.

Zoffany returned late in 1779 to London. His *Tribuna* was seen by Horace Walpole on 12 November. Zoffany may have hoped to finish the picture by March 1774, but work on it had been interrupted by other commissions. As Queen Charlotte's painter Zoffany was granted facilities normally denied to less privileged artists wishing to copy in the Tribuna. The Grand Duke asked the Director of the Gallery to provide Zoffany with all the assistance he needed; and Lord Cowper, who had settled in Florence many years earlier, received the Queen's commands to do everything possible to help the painter: 'he has uncom-

mon Merit & has distinguish'd himself very much in his stile of Portrait Painting'.

Zoffany was given permission to have any picture he wished to copy taken down: even Titian's *Venus of Urbino*, prominently displayed in the foreground of his picture, which had become so popular with copyists that the Grand Duke had decreed that it should not be taken off the walls in future, although serious students were allowed the use of ladders or a scaffold. It was made available to Zoffany on 24 November 1771.[1] Granted such rare privileges, Zoffany did not hesitate to bring into *his* Tribuna works of art from other parts of the Grand-ducal collections and thereby to create a richer anthology of the riches of the Medici collections than was implied in the Queen's original commission. He varied the disposition of the works of art on the shelves; scattered a range of objects on the floor; and brought in at least one important statue, *Cupid and Psyche*, from elsewhere in the Gallery. The arrangement of pictures on the walls differs considerably from the actual lay-out at that time. Seven of the pictures recorded by Zoffany were then hanging in the Pitti and, although he gives a lively impression of the varied surfaces of the works of art and of the styles of the different painters represented, the actual scale of such large paintings as Allori's *Miracle of St Julian* and Rubens's *Horrors of War* has been dramatically distorted so that they can appear to be hanging in the room.

Zoffany had probably painted by the end of 1772 much of the background of the scene in which the figures were to be placed; the three main groups of figures (two of them admiring statues, the third concentrating on the Titian) had been composed by the middle of February 1773; but he made from time to time important alterations, both to figures and works of art, which are discernible by X-ray. For example, Lord Lewisham and his companion, Mr Stevenson, were not incorporated into the group on the left until late in 1777. This group was also radically altered by Zoffany in order to insert himself, holding up Raphael's 'Niccolini-Cowper' *Madonna* for inspection by Lord Cowper and his neighbours: an episode in the composition which underscores the paean to Raphael which echoes through Zoffany's Tribuna and was perhaps designed to assist Cowper in ingratiating himself with the King by providing him with an opportunity (of which he sadly did not avail himself) to acquire a Raphael for his own collection. In the same way the prominent display, unframed, near an apparently casually arranged

[1] Information kindly provided by Mary Webster.

26

selection of Roman, Greek, Etruscan and Egyptian works of art, on the floor of the Tribuna, of Guercino's *Samian Sibyl*, which the Grand Duke did not acquire until early in 1777, may have been a flattering allusion to the King's recent purchase of the painter's *Libyan Sibyl* (No.27).

The most significant innovation which Zoffany made to the Queen's commission was to use the Tribuna as a setting for a highly original conversation-piece, peopled by some of the Englishmen (and Scotsmen) who had visited Florence while he was there and had been entertained by Sir Horace Mann, the British Envoy Extraordinary who had helped to make practical arrange-

ments for Zoffany to work in the Uffizi. Mann thought the picture 'too much crouded with (for the most part) uninteresting Portraits of English travellers then here'; but Zoffany's ability to catch a likeness was often praised and for posterity his picture is an unsurpassed record of the Florentine stage in the general experience of the Grand Tour. When the picture was finally shown at the Royal Academy in 1780 (60), 'the flock of travelling boys, and one does not know or care whom' was criticized by Walpole and was apparently considered by the King to be an 'improper' intrusion on the scene; but Zoffany's industry and imitative skill were universally admired. It

Key

Portraits

1 George, 3rd Earl Cowper (1738–89), Prince of the Holy Roman Empire. A distinguished collector and devoted lover of Florence.

2 Sir John Dick (1720–1804), Baronet of Braid. British Consul at Leghorn, 1754–76. He is wearing his badge as a Baronet of Nova Scotia and the ribbon and star of the Russian order of St Anne of Schleswig-Holstein; he was nominated 'Chevalier' of the order on 25 March 1774 and received the ensigns early in 1775.

3 Other Windsor, 6th Earl of Plymouth (1751–99). He was in Florence in January, February and June 1772.

4 Johann Zoffany.

5 Charles Loraine-Smith (1751–1835), second son of Sir Charles Loraine, 3rd Bt. He left Florence with Mr Doughty (16) on 14 February 1773.

6 Richard Edgcumbe, later 2nd Earl of Mount Edgcumbe (1764–1839).

7 Mr Stevenson, companion to Lord Lewisham (8) on his travels.

8 George Legge, Lord Lewisham, later 3rd Earl of Dartmouth (1755–1810). Lord of the Bedchamber to the Prince of Wales, 1782–3; Lord Chamberlain, 1804–10. He embarked on a tour of the Continent with Mr Stevenson in July 1775. They were in Florence on 2 December 1777.

9 *Called* Joseph Leeson, Viscount Russborough, 2nd Earl of Milltown (1730–1801). His presence in Florence is only reported in the *Gazzetta Toscana* of 8 August 1778, after Zoffany's departure; and the figure does not agree in age or appearance with the portrait by Batoni (1751) in the National Gallery of Ireland.

10 Valentine Knightley (1744–96), of Fawsley. He is probably the Knightley who was in Florence in November 1772; and could well be the Knightley who left Florence in March or April 1773.

11 Pietro Bastianelli, a *custode* in the Gallery.

12 John Gordon. The *Gazzetta Toscana* reported on 2 July 1774 that a *sig. Gordon* was in Florence; he was probably identical with *Monsieur Godron Uffiziale Inghilese*, reported in Florence on 13 August 1774.

13 George Finch, 9th Earl of Winchilsea (1752–1826). Gentleman of the Bedchamber, 1777–1812; Groom of the Stole, 1804–12. He was in Florence from December 1772 to late March 1773.

14 Mr Wilbraham (see No.21 below).

15 Mr Watts. He was reported in Florence on 2 January 1773.

16 Mr Doughty. He was in Florence in February 1773 and left with Loraine-Smith (5) on 14 February.

17 Hon. Felton Hervey (1712–73), ninth son of the 1st Earl of Bristol. Equerry to Queen Caroline of Ansbach and Groom of the Bedchamber to William, Duke of Cumberland. He was in Florence early in September 1772.

18 Thomas Patch (*c*.1725–1782). Painter of caricatures and topographical views. Active in Florence from 1755 until his death.

19 Sir John Taylor (*d*.1786). Recorded in Rome in 1773; perhaps also the Taylor who was in Florence in November 1772.

20 Sir Horace Mann (1706–86). Famous as the friend and correspondent of Horace Walpole. Early in 1738 he was assisting the British Resident at the court of the Grand Duke of Tuscany and in 1740 he succeeded to the post; he stayed at Florence for another forty-six years, as Resident, 1740–65, Envoy Extraordinary, 1765–82, and Envoy Extraordinary and Plenipotentiary, 1782–6. He received the Order of the Bath in 1768.

21 T. Wilbraham. The two gentlemen of this name (see above, No.14) were perhaps two of the sons of Roger Wilbraham of Nantwich: Thomas (*b*.1751), George (1741–1813) or Roger Wilbraham (1743–1829). The two Mr Wilbrahams are reported in Florence by Lord Winchilsea (13) between December 1772 and 16 February 1773.

22 James Bruce (1730–94). The famous African traveller; he was in Florence in January 1774.

Paintings

23 Annibale Carracci. *Bacchante.*

24 Guido Reni. *Charity.*

25 Raphael. *Madonna della Sedia.*

26 Correggio. *Virgin and Child.*

27 Sustermans. *Galileo.*

28 Unidentified. Conceivably the old copy (in the Uffizi) of Rembrandt's *Holy Family* in the Louvre.

29 School of Titian. *Madonna and Child with St Catherine.*

30 Raphael. *St John.*

31 Guido Reni. *The Madonna.*

32 Raphael. *Madonna del Cardellino.*

33 Rubens. *Horrors of War.*

34 Franciabigio. *Madonna del Pozzo.*

35 Holbein. *Sir Richard Southwell.*

36 Lorenzo di Credi. *Portrait of Verrocchio*; now described as a portrait of Perugino by Raphael.

37 Now attributed to Niccolò Soggi. *Holy Family.*

38 Guido Reni. *Cleopatra.*

39 Rubens. *The Painter with Lipsius and his pupils.*

40 Raphael. *Leo X with Cardinals de' Medici and de' Rossi.*

41 Pietro da Cortona. *Abraham and Hagar.* Now in the Kunsthistorisches Museum, Vienna.

42 School of Caravaggio. *The Tribute Money.*

43 Cristofano Allori. *The Miracle of St Julian.*

44 Unidentified. *The Roman Charity.*

45 Raphael. 'Niccolini-Cowper' *Madonna*, formerly at Panshanger and now in Washington.

46 Guercino. *The Samian Sibyl.*

47 Titian. *The Venus of Urbino.*

Of these Nos.24, 25, 27, 29, 33, 38, 39, 42, 43 and 46 are now in the Pitti; Nos.25, 32 and 42 are still in the same frames as those painted by Zoffany.

Statues

48 The *Arrotino* or *Scita Scorticatore.*

49 *Cupid and Psyche.*

50 *The Satyr with the Cymbals.*

51 *Hercules strangling the Serpent.*

52 *The Wrestlers.*

53 *The Venus de' Medici.*

Objects on the Floor

54 South Italian or Apulian *cratere*, 4th century B.C.

55 Etruscan helmet.

56 The Etruscan Chimera.

57, 58, 59 Roman *lucernae.*

60 Egyptian Ptahmose, XVIIIth dynasty.

61 Greek bronze torso.

62 Bust of Julius Caesar.

63 Silver shield of the Consul Flavius Ardaburius Aspar.

64 Bronze head of Antinous.

65 South Italian *cratere.*

66 Etruscan jug.

67 South Italian *situla.*

Nos.54, 55, 56, 60, 61, 63, 64, 65, 66, 67 are in the Museo Archeologico in Florence; No.57 is in the Bargello; and No.62 in the Uffizi.

Objects on the Shelves
(Many remain unidentified)

68 Bust of 'Plautilla'.

69 Small female head.

70 Head of Tiberius in jaspar, on gold mount of the sixteenth century.

71 Bust of 'Annius Verus'.

72 Bust of an unknown boy, the 'Young Nero'.

73 Bronze figure of Hercules.

74 Small Egyptian figure.

75 Bronze *Arion* by Bertoldo di Giovanni.

No.75 is in the Bargello; Nos.69, 70, 74 are in the Museo degli Argenti; No.73 is in the Museo Archeologico; and Nos.68, 71, 72 are in the Uffizi.

76 Octagonal table made by Ligozzi and Poccetti, now in the Opeficio delle Pietre Dure in Florence.

could be claimed that Zoffany's picture, painted with a fresh touch and unflagging energy, provides 'the last visual record of the Tribuna at a time when it still played its original part in the arrangements in the Gallery as a whole' (for useful material on the history of the Tribuna and its contents, see the catalogue, *Mostra Storica della Tribuna degli Uffizi* (Florence, 1970–71), *Quaderni degli Uffizi*, I).

To the earlier accounts of the picture (e.g., in Millar, No.1211) should be added the Princess Royal's letter, written in May 1790 to her brother Augustus, who was travelling in Italy, in which she hopes he will let her know whether, after he has seen the Gallery in Florence, he thinks Zoffany's picture 'like' (M. Webster, *Johan Zoffany*, National Portrait Gallery (1977), No.76); Zoffany's Mr Gordon can now be identified with John Gordon, whose distinguished collection belonged later to the Rev. William Gordon at Saxlingham in Norfolk; and the journal of Robert Harvey includes an account of a visit to the Tribuna on 9 August 1773, when he describes Zoffany's picture: 'the most curious thing in this Tribune & perhaps in all Italy for its nature' in which 'abt a dozen englishmen who were in Florence at that time are likewise drawn in it'. They included Felton Hervey, 'to be talking to Sir Horace Mann altho' [he] is not yet painted' (A.W. Moore, *Norfolk & The Grand Tour*, Norfolk Museums Service (1985), pp.17, 66, 153–4, No.109). Much has been written recently on the 'disguised content' of Zoffany's composition. For an introduction to the attempts to approach the artist's work 'as something more than renderings of empirically observed reality, innocent of anything other than surface meaning' and for direction to the writings of Ronald Paulson (1969 and 1975), the reader is referred to W.L. Pressly, 'Genius Unveiled: The Self-Portraits of Johan Zoffany', *The Art Bulletin*, vol.LXIX, No.1 (New York, March 1987). For the views expressed therein there is no contemporary evidence; and they are sometimes put forward (occasionally by those who have never actually seen the picture) in defiance of statements based on proven facts or unbiased observation.

Giovanni Francesco Barbieri, called *Guercino* (1591–1666)

27 The Libyan Sibyl

Oil on canvas: $45\frac{1}{2} \times 37\frac{1}{4}$ in., 115.6 × 94.6 cm. Inscribed, on the book: *SYBILLA LIBIA*. Acquired by George

27

III, and probably among the works of art purchased for the King by Richard Dalton in Italy in the 1760s, when the newly acquired Buckingham House was being fitted up. The Guercino was placed in the Warm Room, in a carefully planned display of Flemish and Italian seventeenth-century pictures (F. Russell, op. cit., p.531). Dalton also secured for the King from the Gennari family in 1763 the celebrated group of drawings by Guercino now in the Print Room at Windsor.

With its soft colours and delicate, feathery touch it is clearly a late work. It may therefore be the picture of the Libyan Sibyl painted for Ippolito Cattani and paid for on 4 December 1651. It was a half-length and had been painted as a pendant to the Samian Sibyl, paid for on the same date, which is probably the picture now in the Uffizi: prominently displayed, indeed, on the floor in No.26 as a new acquisition. There is a considerable *pentimento* in the outline of the dress on the left shoulder of the figure (Levey, No.521; D. Mahon, *Il Guercino . . . Dipinti*, Palazzo dell'Archiginnasio, Bologna (1968), No.91).

28

Giovanni Antonio Canal, called *Canaletto* (*1697–1768*)

28 **The Bacino di S. Marco with the Bucintoro at the Molo on Ascension Day**

Oil on canvas: $30\frac{1}{4} \times 49\frac{3}{8}$ in., 76.8×125.4 cm. The companion piece to No.25, painted, probably *c*.1734, to record the traditional Marriage with the Sea on Ascension Day: a ceremony which celebrated the naval victory (*c*.998) over the Dalmatians and the presentation of a ring by Pope Alexander III in 1178 to the Doge in gratitude for his part in the reconciliation between the Papacy and Frederick Barbarossa. In No.28 the richly decorated Bucintoro, designed by Stefano Conti, has returned to the Molo after the ceremony at the mouth of the Lido, where the ring was cast into the sea as a symbol of the union between Venice and the Adriatic. Some of the spectators are in carnival dress and a market is being held on the Piazzetta.

Canaletto produced (again, not unmindful of a prototype by Carlevaris) a number of variants on the two main stages of the event, with very little alteration to the architectural background, but considerable variations in scale. A particularly magnificent, slightly earlier, treatment of the theme is in the Crespi collection in Milan (*Canaletto Disegni – Dipinti – Incisioni* (Fondazione Cini, Venice, 1982), No.84). In No.28 the placing of the vessels and smaller boats is particularly subtle, and there is an intriguing use of light and shadow on the boats and their occupants in the foreground. In both the festival pictures painted for Smith the eye is entranced by Canaletto's lively touch and sparkling colour, and in the middle distance, notably in the market scene in No.28, by his evocation, in a brilliant shorthand and with a range of subtle tones, of everyday life in Venice (Levey, No.397; QG, 1980–1, p.21, No.20; J.G. Links, op. cit., p.74; A. Corboz, op. cit., vol.II, P.81).

Sir Thomas Lawrence (1769–1830)

**29 William Cavendish, 6th Duke of Devonshire
(1790–1858)**

Oil on panel: $30 \times 24\frac{1}{2}$ in., 76.2×62.2 cm. Among the portraits bespoken by George IV from Lawrence in 1825 at £187. 10s. Lawrence reported that the portrait was finished by 25 November 1828. He was paid for it on 13 December. G. Morant's account for the frame (£25. 10s.) is dated 20 November.

The Duke was the son of the 5th Duke and the famous Duchess, Georgiana. One of George IV's 'personal and attached friends', he had borne the Orb at the King's Coronation. In 1826 he went as Ambassador Extraordinary to St Petersburg for the Coronation of the Tsar, Nicholas I. Lord Chamberlain, 1827–8, 1830–4, he bore the Curtana at Queen Victoria's Coronation. In Lawrence's portrait the fur-lined coat, worn over the Duke's Windsor uniform and partly hiding his Garter star, possibly alludes to the trip to Russia. The combination of panache and ease is characteristic of Lawrence: a reminder of why his work appealed so strongly to George IV. Sir William Knighton, who knew the King and the painter extremely well, described 'the Power He had of putting down on Canvass the most unexceptionable part of the Face & still preserving the likeness . . . hence the pleasure & satisfaction that all His Portraits gave to his employers'. The Duke, a man of conspicuous charm, carried out extensive alterations and additions at Chatsworth which he described in his *Handbook*. The brilliant handling and lustrous surface of Lawrence's portrait are interesting premonitions of the Duke's patronage, a few years later, of Landseer (Millar, No.895).

Jean-Baptiste Greuze (1725–1805)

30 Silence!

Oil on canvas: $24\frac{5}{8} \times 20$ in., 62.5×50.8 cm; the original painted area is $23\frac{3}{4} \times 19\frac{1}{2}$ in., 60.3×49.5 cm. Purchased in Paris in 1817 by Lord Yarmouth for the Prince Regent. Originally in the collection of Jean de Julienne in Paris and lent by him to the Salon of 1759 (103), when a critic described it as '*plein d'esprit*'. Thereafter in the de Montulé and marquis de Vaudreuil collections in Paris (sold respectively in 1783 and 1787); sold in the Stanley sale in London, 7 June 1815.

29

In this finely preserved example of Greuze's domestic scenes, a very young mother asks her eldest son not to blow his small trumpet and thereby wake the baby, who has fallen asleep at his mother's breast, or the slightly older child asleep in his little chair, on which hangs a drum which the oldest child has probably already broken. Greuze made a number of drawings in preparation for the composition; a preparatory drawing for the oldest boy was sold at Christie's, 4 July 1984 (120). Edgar Munhall (see below, p.102) has suggested that in such subjects Greuze revealed his interest in contemporary theories about the upbringing of children and in the need to correct, at an early age, 'minor transgressions' which could foreshadow 'graver faults'. There is perhaps the same underlying preoccupation in *L'Enfant Gâté*, on almost the same scale, in The Hermitage. Anita Brookner (see below, pp.9, 16, 33), discussing *Sensibilité* in the literary field, stresses the importance that such writers as Toussaint or Moissy attached to breast-feeding: 'this most tender of functions'.

30

No.30 was painted during the artist's most productive and contented years, when he enjoyed, moreover, a great reputation for his unique ability to move the spectator with his treatment of simple manners and everyday emotions. No.30 is Greuze's masterpiece within a tradition established by Dutch and Flemish genre painters of the previous century, whose work was so enormously admired at the time. It illustrates the synthesis of themes derived from those painters, with an enjoyment of sentiment, which creates the mood of *sensibilité*; and it is of considerable significance as an indication of the old-fashioned, basically French-inspired, tastes of such connoisseurs as Lord Hertford and George IV and of their admiration for eighteenth-century French, and earlier Dutch, painting. Anita Brookner cites a painting by Maes, formerly in the Grand-ducal collection in Weimar, as a possible prototype for the story in No.30 (Anita Brookner, *Greuze* (1972), pp.60, 98, 100; E. Munhall, *Jean-Baptiste Greuze*, Wadsworth Atheneum, Hartford (1976–7), pp.14–15, No.23).

PLATE VII
Detail from *A Woman at her Toilet*
by Jan Steen (No.36)

31

*Elisabeth-Louise Vigée-Lebrun
(1755–1842)*

31 Charles-Alexandre de Calonne (1734–1802)
COLOUR PLATE VIII (detail) opposite

Oil on canvas: 59 × 50½ in., 149.9 × 128.3 cm. Signed and
dated: *Le Brun.1784*. The sitter was *Contrôleur-Général
des Finances* to Louis XVI. Unable to push through his

plans for restoring the solvency of Louis XVI's government, he was dismissed in 1787 and retired to England. In
1789 he joined the *émigrés*. He was compelled to sell in
London in 1795 his fine collection of pictures in order to
settle the liabilities incurred in support of the exiles. His
conviction that the French Revolution represented a
threat to every established government was fully shared
by George IV, who acquired No.31 in or before 1806. It is
therefore one of the Prince of Wales's finest early
acquisitions. It is also one of the painter's most accomplished portraits, a lively and sympathetic presentation of
a prominent figure in government on the eve of the
French Revolution: seated, in a beautiful black silk suit,

PLATE VIII
Detail from *Charles-Alexandre de Calonne*
by Elisabeth-Louise Vigée-Lebrun (No.31)

enriched with ribbon and star of the Order of the Saint-Esprit, at a table on which are books, an *encrier* and a bill; holding a message addressed to the King and resting his arm on some official papers. The table is a fine example of the *style Louis XVI* in contrast to the equally grand, but more old-fashioned, chair.

The *Édit* on the table is dated *aout 1784*. The artist recorded in her *Souvenirs* that she had painted a portrait of Calonne which was shown at the Salon in 1785 (87). The three-quarter-length format prompted Mlle Arnoult to exclaim: '*Madame Le Brun lui a coupé les jambes, afin qu'il reste en place*'. The artist was harassed with unpleasant rumours about the payment for the portrait and with allegations that she was having an affair with her sitter. She stated that she received 4,000 francs in payment; and in fact she considered Calonne anything but attractive: chiefly because he wore '*une perruque fiscale*', which offended her sense of the picturesque. She wrote also that she had rushed the portrait through so fast that she did not, contrary to her normal practice, paint the hands from life. Her husband asserted that for the portrait Calonne paid 3,600 *livres* placed in a snuff-box valued at 1,200 *livres* at the most (*Souvenirs* (Paris, 1835), vol.I, pp.105, 111, 332–3; *The Eye of Thomas Jefferson*, ed. W.H. Adams, National Gallery of Art, Washington (1976), No.227).

Thomas Gainsborough (1727–88)

32 James Quin (1693–1766)

Oil on canvas: 25½ × 20 in., 64.8 × 50.8 cm. Almost certainly cut from a larger canvas, and probably when it was decided that the sitter should be painted at full-length. No.32 therefore precedes the full-length in the National Gallery of Ireland which was exhibited by Gainsborough at the Society of Artists in 1763 (41), when it was much admired: 'of uncommon force and vigour, with a truth and animation beyond Mr. Gainsborough's usual performance'. The head in No.32 has been completed, *ad vivum* and with a lively touch, with a first indication of the tone of the background, and upon a reddish-fawn underpainting. Quin was living in retirement in Bath when he sat to Gainsborough. It is not known when the portrait entered the Royal Collection. It was probably the portrait of Quin which was among the unfinished portraits, the property of the artist's widow, in his nephew Dupont's sale at Christie's, 10 April 1797 (17). In the Royal Collection it was first recorded at

32

Buckingham Palace in 1876. The acquisitions made by George IV and Queen Victoria are recorded in almost infallible detail; as the portrait of Quin is nowhere mentioned as having been acquired by either of them, it could be suggested that it entered the collection between 1830 and 1837.

Quin first appeared on the stage in Dublin, but by 1715 was acting in London, where he gave his last performance in 1751. A notable Shakespearean actor, he was a celebrated Falstaff. In January 1749 he had directed the royal children in a performance of *Cato* in front of their parents at Leicester House and he claimed to have given the young George III lessons in elocution (Millar, No.803). Gainsborough's presentation of Quin recalls Hogarth's rather assertive image (Tate Gallery) painted some twenty years earlier.

33

Johan Zoffany (1733–1810)

33 John Cuff and his Assistant

Oil on canvas: $35\frac{1}{4} \times 27\frac{1}{4}$ in., 89.5 × 69.2 cm. Signed and dated: *Zoffanÿ pinx/1772*. Purchased by, or painted for, George III or Queen Charlotte and recorded in Princess Augusta's Bedroom at Kew as 'A Mathematitian. Zoffani'. It had been exhibited at the Royal Academy in 1772 (291): *An optician, with his attendant*. Apart from its brilliant painterly quality, revealed in the recent cleaning and restoration, the composition displays the remarkable skill and lively sympathy in recording people and a multitude of objects in a given setting which the artist had first demonstrated in his stage pictures, and in the conversation-pieces he had painted for the royal family, and of which he was to give a virtuoso display in No.26. It is also rare as a picture of a London craftsman actually at work at his bench surrounded by the tools and materials of his trade. Horace Walpole, in a typically perverse judgement, criticized those qualities in the work which in fact render it so remarkable: 'Extremely natural, but the characters too common nature, and the chiaroscuro

34

destroyed by his servility in imitating the reflexions of the glasses'.

On the strength of a note in an inventory drawn up in the time of George III, and the identification of the sitter when the picture was exhibited at the British Institution in 1814 (79), the craftsman has been identified as John Cuff, the optician, whose shop, 'at the sign of the Reflecting Microscope', was near Serjeant's Inn Gate in Fleet Street. He perfected inventions and important improvements in microscopes and made instruments for George III and Queen Charlotte. Celina Fox, however, has recently cast doubt on this identification, chiefly on the grounds that by the time the picture was painted Cuff had been declared bankrupt and had no shop and no money. On the other hand in 1770 and 1771 payments were made on the King's behalf to provide 'Mr. Cuffe' with such materials as a diamond, grinding tools, emery and six chucks for his lathe (RA, Geo. 16826).

The reason for the addition made by Zoffany, during painting, to the bottom of the canvas is not clear. It is possible that the original canvas had been damaged very early and had to be repaired by the painter; but it is more likely that in the course of painting Zoffany realized that elements in the design were coming too close to the bottom edge and that he would have to enlarge his canvas. The *pentimenti* above (in the perspective of the window, the position of the bench, in the figure of the assistant and the lower half of Cuff himself) are not so significant as to suggest a substantial re-working of the composition (Millar, No.1209; M. Webster, *Johan Zoffany*, National Portrait Gallery (1977), No.71; C. Fox, *Londoners*, Museum of London (1987), pp.111, 266).

Willem van de Velde the Younger (1633–1707)

34 A Calm: a States Yacht under Sail, close to the Shore, with many other Vessels

Oil on panel: $23\frac{1}{2} \times 28$ in., 59.6×71.2 cm. Acquired by George IV with the Baring collection in 1814: a purchase which enriched his collection with a group of works of exceptional quality. Formerly in the Smeth van Alphen collection in Amsterdam, sold in 1810.

Probably painted c.1655. The yacht reappears in a number of pictures, among them a second *Calm* in the Royal Collection (White, No.213) which is signed and dated 1659 and in which the yacht is shown with a later rig

(on the stern of the yacht are the lion supporters to the Orange arms). No.34 was painted, therefore, some eighteen years before Van de Velde and his father settled in England, where they were taken into royal service and may be said to have founded the British school of marine painting.

No.34 lacks the dramatic sense of composition and obviously painterly qualities of the painter's English works; but it is a work of a tranquil beauty (and in a marvellous state of preservation), a quintessential example of the kind of picture by Van de Velde which collectors in the eighteenth century were to pursue so keenly. Much of its poetic charm lies in the qualities it shares with the beach scenes by Van de Velde's brother Adriaen (e.g., No.53) in which the low horizon and the soft, clear light create an atmosphere of rare subtlety. The figures which, in the foreground, contribute so much to the mood of the picture, may well have been painted by Adriaen (White, No.212; *The Art of the Van de Veldes*, National Maritime Museum (1982), No.25).

Rembrandt van Rijn (1606–69)

35 Christ and the Magdalen at the Tomb; 'Noli Me Tangere'

Oil on panel: $24 \times 19\frac{1}{2}$ in., 61×49.5 cm. Signed and dated: *Rembrandt.f.../1638*. Painted for the Amsterdam precentor and '*ziekentrooster*', H.F. Waterloos. A poem on the picture, written by Jeremias de Decker, was published in 1660 and a copy of his lines is attached to the back of the panel. The picture has a most distinguished subsequent history: bought from Willem van der Goes in Leiden by Valerius Röver of Delft, 1721; sold by his widow to Wilhelm VIII, Landgrave of Hesse-Cassel for the Gallery at Cassel; taken in 1806 from Cassel by the Napoleonic Governor of Hesse and later owned by the Empress Josephine at Malmaison; acquired by Lafontaine, probably from Eugène de Beauharnais; and secured in 1819 by George IV who gave Lafontaine four pictures in exchange. It and No.22 are the only great religious pictures which the King acquired.

Rembrandt has taken as his text St John's account, xx, 10–15, and illustrates the moment when the Magdalen 'turned herself back, and saw Jesus standing'. Christ's large hat indicates that he is still seen as the gardener. The potentially intensely dramatic encounter, the presence of the angels, the dawn over the distant buildings which, as Christopher White (see below) has pointed out, recall

35

Rembrandt's drawings of seemingly English medieval buildings, and the two figures leaving the garden, combine to create, in Gerson's words, 'a marvellous vision' (op. cit., p.82). Between 1631 and 1639 Rembrandt had painted a number of small pictures of the Passion. In these, as in many other paintings, drawings and etchings, he proved himself to be, among Protestant painters, the most moving interpreter of the Bible, partly because the mood of his narrative is so unforced. When he was at work for the Prince of Orange on the series of scenes of the Passion, Rembrandt had written (on 12 January 1639) that he had expressed in two of them the 'deepest and most innate emotion'. In compositional terms – in lay-out and in scale – No.35 is close (in reverse) to the *Visitation* in Detroit (ibid., 203). Two drawings by Rembrandt in the Rijksmuseum can be associated with No.35 (White, No.161).

Jan Steen (1626–79)

36 A Woman at her Toilet

COLOUR PLATE VII (detail) facing page 48

Oil on panel: $25\frac{1}{2} \times 20$ in., 64.7×53 cm. Signed and dated: *JSteen* (initials in monogram) *1663*. Acquired by George IV from Delahante in 1821. Formerly in the Fiers Kappeyne collection in Amsterdam (sold in 1775) and in the Verhulst collection in Brussels (sold in 1779).

The exceptional quality of the picture, painted when Steen was living in Haarlem and producing his finest work, the beauty of the colour and the liquid touch which seems so vividly to sustain the wit with which Steen tells a story, would have appealed to George IV. It is an interesting commentary on the esteem in which Dutch painters were held early in the nineteenth century that Smith (1833) could give no higher praise to No.36 than to describe it as 'finished with the neatness and delicacy of the best works of F. Mieris'. Mrs Jameson also (1844) thought the choice of subject, the 'elegance of the execution' and the colouring 'which resembles Mieris', unusual for Steen.

George IV would also have been amused by the theme of the picture, even if he would not have taken in the subtler allusions with which Steen points the moral therein. These are set out by Christopher White (see below). That the young woman is a wanton is made plain by the disorder in her dress and bed; by the presence of the dog ('traditional companion of courtesans'); by the box of jewels open to show a necklace of pearls; and by the equivocal action of pulling on a stocking. The pervading theme is the transitoriness of life, beauty and the delights of physical love, a theme stressed in the head of the cherub in the centre of the swag carved over the arched doorway from which we look down into the bedroom (a setting unusually elaborate in Steen's *œuvre*); in the vine tendril which covers the skull; and in the broken string of the lute, which can be read as an allusion to the loss of virginity (White, No.189).

36

37

Adriaen van de Velde (1636–72)

37 A Hawking Party setting out

Oil on canvas: $19\frac{7}{8} \times 18\frac{3}{4}$ in., 50.5×47.6 cm. Signed and dated: *A.V. Velde f/1666*. Bought by Lord Yarmouth for George IV at Lord Rendlesham's sale by Coxe, 28 May 1810 (32); formerly in the Choiseul-Praslin and Van Helsleuter collections in Paris (sold in 1793 and 1802 respectively).

One of the artist's comparatively rare hunting scenes. The allusions to different aspects of the chase – the hounds, the sporting gun, the hunting-horn and the hoop of hawks – would have pleased George IV, whose love of field sports explains many of his purchases and much of his patronage. The 'radiance of a fine summer's morning', in Smith's words (1834), has seldom been more brilliantly depicted than in this 'beautiful work of rare excellence'. The range of tones and quality of brushwork are, throughout, of exceptional refinement (White, No.206).

39

Fra Angelico *(c.1400–55)*

38 Saint Peter Martyr

Tempera on panel: $10 \times 4\frac{3}{4}$ in., 25.5×12.2 cm. In the collection, in Florence, of Johann Metzger (d.1844). Acquired, presumably from his son Ludwig, by Gruner on behalf of Prince Albert in 1845. Gruner was paid £89. 12s. 9d. on 30 May 1845 for '2 Pictures'. Nos.38 and 39 were placed, with a number of his finest early pictures, in the Prince's Dressing- and Writing-Room at Osborne.

John Shearman has drawn attention to the beautiful quality of the head and the delicate play of light and shade across the drapery. The panel was probably painted as one of a series set into the flanking pilasters of an altarpiece (Shearman, No.8).

Benozzo Gozzoli *(c.1421–97)*

39 The Fall of Simon Magus

Tempera on panel: $9\frac{5}{8} \times 13\frac{5}{8}$ in., 24.3×34.5 cm. Presumably acquired in Italy in the last years of the eighteenth century by William Young Ottley. In a group of four pictures bought from his brother, Warner Ottley, by Prince Albert on 14 July 1846. For No.39 the Prince paid £25.

One of five surviving predella panels from the altarpiece, *The Virgin and Child enthroned among Angels and Saints* in the National Gallery, which Gozzoli, on 23 October 1461, contracted to paint for the oratory of the Compagnia di Sta Maria della Purificazione e di S. Zanobi in Florence. In the contract it is stated that the painter should paint the predella himself and not assign the task to an

assistant: hence its fine, jewel-like quality, vivid characterization and sense of narrative. There is an account in the
Golden Legend of the episode depicted. The Emperor
Nero is seated on the left. On the right are St Peter and
St Paul. Simon Magus had determined to prove to Nero
that he was superior to St Peter by launching himself on
the way to Heaven from the top of a tower; St Peter,
provoked by the Emperor, commands the demons supporting the sorcerer to let him fall. There is a noticeable
possible *pentimento* on the wall behind the Emperor's
head (Shearman, No.132).

Albrecht Dürer (1471–1528)

40 Portrait of Burkard von Speyer

Oil (see below) on panel: $12\frac{1}{2} \times 10\frac{1}{4}$ in., 31.7×26 cm. This
includes a narrow tapering addition on left and right. The
original painted surface is $12\frac{1}{2} \times 10/10\frac{1}{8}$ in., $31.7 \times$
$25.4/25.7$ cm. Signed and dated: *1506 AD* (initials in
monogram). On the back of the panel is Charles I's brand
and the picture is recorded by Van der Doort as hanging
in the Chair Room at Whitehall, in which the King had
placed some of his most precious and finely wrought small
pictures. Close to No.40, for example, hung Dürer's *Self-
portrait*, now in the Prado, and the portrait of his father in
the National Gallery. When the King's possessions were
dispersed after his death, No.40 was sold for £60 to Ralph
Grynder and others (it was recovered at the Restoration).
It is interesting to note that the *Self-portrait* and the
portrait of the artist's father were valued together at £100.

Painted during Dürer's second visit to Venice, 1506–7.
On 23 September 1506 he wrote from Venice to
Pirkheimer that he would be ready to leave Venice in
about a month's time, 'but I must first take the portraits of
some people I have promised'. No.40 may have been
among them. The sitter has been recognized, almost
certainly rightly, among the votive figures (he appears
fourth from the left in the composition) in the celebrated
Brotherhood of the Rosary or *Feast of the Rose Garlands*
(now in the National Gallery in Prague) which in 1506
Dürer was commissioned to paint for S. Bartolommeo,
the church, near the Fondaco dei Tedeschi, with which
the German colony in Venice was associated. The
congregation in the painting were members of the colony.
The young man here has been identified as Burkard von
Speyer (of whom nothing is known) on the basis of a
miniature portrait, dated 1506, in the Schlossmuseum at
Weimar. A comparison of the portrait with No.5, painted

40

at almost exactly the same date, reveals something of
Dürer's admiration for Bellini, whose influence is so
strongly felt in the altarpiece and of whom Dürer wrote
while he was in Venice: 'I am really friendly with him. He
is very old, but is still the best painter of them all'. There
is a charming account by Cammermeister, in his preface
to a Latin translation of Dürer's work on human proportions, of a conversation between the two painters in
the course of which Bellini, who particularly admired the
fineness and delicacy with which Dürer painted hairs,
asked if he would give him one of the brushes with which
he drew them. It transpired that he used exactly the same
kind of brush as Bellini. With one of them, to Bellini's
incredulous wonderment, he drew some long, wavy
tresses (*The Writings of Albrecht Dürer*, translated and ed
by W.M. Conway (edn of 1958), pp.138–9). No.40 is the
only portrait in oils in the British Isles universally
considered to be by Dürer.

Cleaning and restoration have demonstrated that the
painting is in a very good state of preservation. There are
some losses round the edges, very small losses in the face

and an old damage in the neck. The type of gesso used is unusual in Venice, but has been noted in a work by Catena. The pale pink underpainting is also unusual. There are *pentimenti* in the edge of the cap over the brow and in the position of the shoulders. Cleaning has clarified the position of the figure in space. In the painting of the face the technique has the appearance of watercolour, quite unlike the technique of northern painters at this date. The shadows on the nose seem to have been softened or thinned by the use of the thumb. The slight blanching in the darks of the hair are caused by the breaking-down of the original medium. Analysis of the media has revealed so far (predominantly) egg, combined with traces of oil, and glue (E. Panofsky, *The Life and Art of Albrecht Dürer* (Princeton, 1955), p.116; M. Levey, *Dürer* (1964), p.75; A. Smith and A.O. della Chiesa, *The Complete Paintings of Dürer* (1968), pp.85, 105, No.118; F. Anzelewesky, *Albrecht Dürer das Malerische Werk* (Berlin, 1971), pp.201–2, No.97).

Lucas Cranach the Elder (1472–1553)

41 Lucretia

41

Oil on panel: $29\frac{7}{8} \times 22\frac{1}{8}$ in., 75.9 × 56.2 cm. Dated: *1530* with the artist's device of a flying snake or dragon. Purchased by Prince Albert on 17 May 1844 for £500 from Nicholls. It was placed by the Prince in the Pages' Waiting-Room at Osborne with other northern pictures, including a number which bore attributions to Cranach and included portraits of the Prince's Saxon ancestors who had been Cranach's most important patrons. The first picture listed in the Prince's 'Rough Catalogue' of his acquisitions is a version of Cranach's portrait of Frederick the Wise, Elector of Saxony, which was brought over from Coburg in 1840.

The story of Lucretia, the virtuous wife of Tarquinius Collatinus who killed herself after she had been ravished by Sextus Tarquinius, is told by Livy, *History of Rome*, book I, 57–59. The subject was frequently painted by Cranach from *c*.1518 (M.J. Friedländer and J. Rosenberg, *Die Gemälde von Lucas Cranach* (Berlin, 1932), p.66, No.198 (b); D. Koepplin and T. Falk, *Lukas Cranach* (Basel, Stuttgart, 1976), vol.II, pp.660–70).

42

Hans Baldung Grien (1484/5–1545)

42 Portrait of a young Man with a Rosary

Oil on panel: $20\frac{1}{4} \times 14\frac{1}{2}$ in., 51.4×36.8 cm. Dated: *.ANNA DÑI.1509*. The date is divided by an arabesque illustrating an owl attacked by a smaller bird, a possible symbol, depending on the identification of the species, of the conflict between day and night or good and evil. Formerly in the collection assembled by Prince Ludwig Kraft Ernst von Oettingen-Wallenstein, who had borrowed money from Prince Albert, but was unable to repay the debt. His pictures were sent to London as a security for the loan and were on show at Kensington Palace. They failed to attract a buyer and eventually became the property of the Prince. No.42 appears as No.283 (as by Herri met de Bles) in the *Grundbuch* (1817–18) of the Oettingen-Wallenstein collection and as one of the pictures acquired from the collection of Count Joseph von Rechberg. When it entered the Royal Collection the portrait was attributed to Hans von Kulmbach.

Painted in the year in which the painter settled in Strasburg, No.42 is his earliest dated single portrait. It already shows a glimpse of the idiosyncratic, almost quirky, mood which characterizes all Baldung's portraits and makes him so arresting an artist in this field (*Hans Baldung Grien*, Staatliche Kunsthalle, Karlsruhe (1959), No.9; *German Art 1400–1800*, City of Manchester Art Gallery (1961), No.77; G. von der Osten, *Hans Baldung Grien* (Berlin, 1983), pp.20, 54–55, No.8).

Quinten Metsys (1465/6–1530)

43 Desiderius Erasmus (1466–1536)

Oil on panel: $19\frac{7}{8} \times 17\frac{3}{4}$ in., 50.4×45 cm. Erasmus is in a panelled interior writing the opening words of his *Paraphrase of St Paul's Epistle to the Romans*, on which he was engaged in May 1517. Metsys produces a plausible imitation of Erasmus's handwriting; and Erasmus is writing with the reed pen he always used. Of the six books on the shelves behind Erasmus, four are inscribed across the page-ends with the titles which made him famous: '*NOVUM TESTAMENT*'; '*ΛΟΥΚΙΑΝΟΣ*'; and '*HIERONYMVS*'. Erasmus's editions of the New Testament and St Jerome (in No.43 the sitter consciously evokes the conventional image of St Jerome in his study) had appeared in 1516; the translations by Sir Thomas More and Erasmus of some of Lucian's *Dialogues* had

43

been first published in 1506; the remaining volume, originally inscribed 'MOR', may have been intended to refer to the *Encomium Moriae*, written when Erasmus was staying with More in 1509 and dedicated to him.

Until recently No.43 was regarded as an inferior version of the portrait in the Galleria Nazionale d'Arte Antica in Rome. The opportunity to study that version in association with Metsys's portrait of Peter Gillis, the town clerk of Antwerp, in the collection of the Earl of Radnor (J.B. Trapp and H.S. Herbrüggen, '*The King's Good Servant*' *Sir Thomas More*, National Portrait Gallery (1977–78), No.53), provoked a re-assessment of the royal version which was shown to be Metsys's original portrait of Erasmus and, with Lord Radnor's panel, which is of precisely the same physical nature, to have formed part of the diptych commissioned by them as a present for More. The two portraits were in the collection of Charles I whose brand is on the back of both panels. Lorne Campbell (see below) provides an excellent resumé of a remarkable piece of collaborative art-historical research in which he, the two authors cited above and Margaret Mann Phillips were involved. The two parts of the diptych were probably separated during the Interregnum.

Technical examination of No.43 revealed that it has probably been reduced in size; alterations were made at a later date to the inscriptions on the books on the shelves; but interesting small changes made in the course of painting have also been noted: in the fingers of the right hand, the painting of the scissors and the pen over what lies behind them, the contours of the right sleeve and the far cheek, and the position of the lower shelf. When, in the imagination, the later additions are removed from the pendant in Lord Radnor's collection, the panels are found to be of identical size and the composition of the backgrounds perfectly aligned.

Of the two portraits, that of Erasmus had been begun by 30 May 1517. Delays were caused in the painting of the portraits by Gillis's illness and by a change in the appearance of Erasmus after he had taken some purgative pills. On 8 September the diptych was dispatched; and on 7 October More wrote to both sitters to thank them for the present. His letter to Gillis contained a description of the two portraits. Professor Trapp (see below) has made the point that in the version in Rome Erasmus's eyes appear as brown, but in No.43, correctly, as grey-blue. He and his colleagues describe the original diptych as 'a pledge of regard and affinity by two great Netherlanders to their great English friend'. The friendship between More and Erasmus had begun in 1499, on Erasmus's first visit to England; during this visit More had taken his friend to Eltham, where he saw the royal children, among them the nine-year-old Prince Henry: 'having already something of royalty in his demeanour, in which there was a certain dignity combined with singular courtesy' (L. Campbell, M.M. Phillips, H.S. Herbrüggen and J.B. Trapp, 'Quintin Matsys, Desiderius Erasmus, Pieter Gillis and Thomas More', *Burl. Mag.*, vol.CXX (1978), pp.716–24; J.B. Trapp, 'A postscript to Matsys', ibid., vol.CXXI (1979), pp.434–7; Campbell, No.54; L. Silver, *The Paintings of Quinten Massys* (1984), pp.105–10, 235–7, Cat.58).

Le Nain

44 The young Card-players

Oil on canvas: $21\frac{5}{8} \times 25\frac{1}{8}$ in., 54.9 × 63.8 cm. Purchased by George IV, when Prince of Wales, at Christie's, 23 March 1803 (48) for £388. 10s. as by 'Carravaggio or Le Nain', stated to have come from the Palazzo Aldobrandini in Rome, and to have been acquired from Castiglione by Thomas Lister Parker who disposed of it to Walsh Porter

The researches of Professor Jacques Thuillier, the fruits of which are presented in the catalogue (see below) of the exhibition in Paris in 1978–9, brought to light much fresh information on the lives of the three brothers Le Nain, Antoine, Louis and Mathieu, and launched a radical reassessment of the approach by which earlier critics had endeavoured to categorize, with misleading precision, the work and personality of the three artists. There is in fact no single surviving work which can be securely attributed to any of the the three brothers and thus form the basis on which an *œuvre* could be built up. Probably born between 1602 and 1610 in Laon, they were all settled by 1633 in Paris and worked closely together there. Antoine and Louis died in 1648; Mathieu survived until 1677.

No.44 has usually been attributed to Mathieu. The alternative attribution to Caravaggio (in 1803) is not without significance; reminiscences of the Bamboccianti in Rome are more obvious in No.44 than in any other work by the brothers. Of the other versions of the composition, the most important is the small version on copper in the Louvre (No.16 in the catalogue cited below) which is painted with a stickier touch and has two additional figures in the background. In colour, and in handling, No.44 is a most sophisticated work. The card-player in the centre, showing a card to the player on his left, is very close in type to the boy cutting bread in the *Three Ages* in the National Gallery (*Les frères Le Nain*, Grand Palais, Paris (1978–9), No.17, with full bibliography; the reviewer of the exhibition in the *Burl. Mag.*, vol.cxx (1978), p.873, links No.44 with *La Tabagie*, signed and dated 1643, in the Louvre; see also A. Blunt, *Art and Architecture in France 1500 to 1700* (edn of 1980), p.432.

Jan van der Heyden (1637–1712)

45 A View of Veere

Oil on panel: 18 × 22 in., 45.7 × 55.9 cm. Signed: *I.V. Heyde*. Purchased by George IV from William Harris in 1811; formerly in the de Selle and Randon de Boisset collections in Paris (sold 1761 and 1777) and the Merens collection in Amsterdam (sold 1778).

The town of Veere is in Zeeland, on the island of Walcheren, looking across the strait to Noord Beveland. It was once an important port, carrying on trade with Scotland. The Groote Kerk, which was to be badly damaged by fire in 1686, can be seen beyond the old walls of the town. Christopher White (see below) cites a number of other views of the town by Van der Heyden. None are dated, but No.45 could perhaps be dated in the early 1660s. The figures, understandably, have been attributed to Adriaen van de Velde. Seymour Slive (*Dutch Art and Architecture 1600 to 1800* (1966), p.193) has analysed well the particular refinement of Van der Heyden's style. Despite his extreme attention to detail, nothing disturbs the overall structure and integrity of the composition: thanks, in part, to a most subtle disposition of light and shade. Van der Heyden's work was important for the view-painters of the eighteenth century. Slive pointed out that 'among eighteenth-century artists one must turn to Canaletto to find his equal'. Sir Joshua Reynolds thought that Van der Heyden's paintings had very much the effect of nature as seen through the *camera obscura*. Critics in the nineteenth century (see S. Alpers, *The Art of Describing* (Chicago, 1983), p.29) compared his work to that of the photographer (White, No.65).

44

45

63

46

Adriaen van Ostade (1610–85)

46 The Interior of a Peasant's Cottage

Oil on panel: 18⅜ × 16⅜ in., 46.7 × 41.6 cm. Signed and dated: *Av.* (in monogram) *Ostade/1668*. Bought for George IV by Lord Yarmouth (apparently before the sale) at the Lafontaine sale, 12 June 1811 (59).

In 1647 Ostade had produced an etching of a peasant woman nursing her child in a similarly 'tumbledown' interior; twenty-one years later he produced, in Robinson's words (see below) 'his most moving portrayal of family affection'. It is also, technically, a masterpiece of genre painting, both in colour and in handling. There is still something of the energy displayed in Ostade's earlier work, when he was under the influence of Brouwer. It is an excellent example of the kind of Dutch genre painting which exercised so profound an influence in France in the eighteenth century on painters, notably Greuze (see

No.30), of pictures of *sensibilité*. In the early nineteenth century Ostade's work was warmly admired. John Smith in the first part of his *Catalogue Raisonné*, published in 1829, went so far as to claim that Ostade's treatment of light 'enabled him to give a charm to his pictures, which no other artist's works possess in an equal degree'. They had a profound influence on a painter such as Wilkie whose pastiches of Dutch and Flemish genre painters of the seventeenth century were popular with the connoisseurs who, in the time of George IV, were so avidly collecting the works of these artists (White, No.132; W. Robinson in *Masters of Seventeenth-Century Dutch Genre Painting*, Philadelphia Museum of Art; Gemälde-galerie, Berlin (West); Royal Academy (1984), No.91).

PLATE IX
Detail from *A Flemish Fair*
by Jan Brueghel (No.52)

64

47

Jan van der Heyden (1637–1712)

47 A Country House on the Vliet near Delft
COLOUR PLATE X (detail) opposite

Oil on panel: $18\frac{1}{2} \times 23\frac{1}{4}$ in., 47×59 cm. Signed: *Heyde*.
Acquired by George IV with the Baring collection in
1814. Formerly in the comte de Vence collection (sold
1761) and the Blondel de Gagny collection (sold 1776),
both in Paris.

PLATE X
Detail from *A Country House on the Vliet near Delft*
by Jan van der Heyden (No.47)

Probably painted *c*.1660. Again, the figures have been
traditionally attributed to Adriaen van de Velde. The
house has recently been identified as the 'Huis Pasgeld,
aan de Haagsche Vaart'. Demolished *c*.1892, it stood near
Delft on the river Vliet. It belonged in the seventeenth
century first to the family of De Hertoghe van Orsmael
and thereafter to Anne de Hertoghe who was married to
Willem van Treslong, probably the owner when No.47
was painted. In 1670 the house passed to the family of
Teding van Berkhout (White, No.66; C. Schmidt, *Om de
Eer van de Familie* (Amsterdam, 1986), pp.74, 83, 212,
215).

48

David Teniers the Younger (1610–90)

48 'Le Tambour Battant'

COLOUR PLATE XIII (detail) between pages 80 and 81

Oil on copper: $19\frac{5}{8} \times 25\frac{3}{4}$ in., 49.8 × 65.4 cm. Signed and dated: *D.TENIERS.F.1647*. Bought by Phillips for the Prince of Wales at the Walsh Porter sale at Christie's, 23 March 1803 (45). Its quality and amusing content would have appealed to the Prince who owned a remarkably fine group of pictures by Teniers; and the martial still life would have given the Prince, who inherited undiluted the Hanoverian enthusiasm for military detail, extra pleasure. The artist records an impression of garrison life in the armies in the Southern Netherlands under the command of the Archduke Leopold-William, for whom he was working at this date and in whose service he was subsequently to be formally enrolled. The drummer is beating his drum outside an officer's quarters into which a page is carrying a bundle wrapped in scarlet cloth. On the wall near the door hang pistols in holsters, a wheel-lock gun and an elaborate target. On the ground are pieces of armour, a flintlock gun and pistol and a powder-horn. The colours in the draped standard are blue, green and red on white. Beyond are tents; an officer and a sergeant; and troops playing cards. A musketeer is on guard on the walls. These elements appear in many variations, signed and dated, for example, 1642, 1644, 1646 and 1652. The long struggle against the Northern Netherlands came to an end early in 1648 with the Treaty of Münster (M. Klinge in *Bruegel Une dynastie de Peintres*, Palais des Beaux-Arts, Brussels (1980), No.210).

Duccio *(c.1255–60–1318 or 1319)*

49 Triptych: Crucifixion and other Subjects

Tempera: central panel: $17\frac{5}{8} \times 12\frac{3}{8}$ in., 44.9 × 31.4 cm, round-headed; spandrel above, with two angels: $5\frac{1}{2} \times 13\frac{3}{4}$ in., 13.9 × 34.9 cm; wings, on the left the Annunciation above the Virgin and Child enthroned, on the right the Stigmatization of St Francis above Christ and the Virgin enthroned: $17\frac{5}{8} \times 6\frac{5}{8}$ in., 44.8 × 16.9 cm. Acquired in Siena by Johann Metzger (d.1844); bought by Prince Albert from Ludwig Metzger in Florence, through Gruner, on 7 April 1846. The Prince paid £190 for the triptych and the *Madonna with Angels*, then ascribed to Fra Angelico, now to Zanobi Strozzi (Shearman, No.252). Both pictures were placed in the Prince's Dressing- and Writing-Room at Osborne.

John Shearman (see below) provides a detailed account of the physical structure and condition of the panels. Probably before it came to England the triptych had been set in a frame with the panels laid out in an open position between mouldings in the same style as those still round the panel ascribed to Strozzi. The panels were restored by Kennedy North after the *Italian Art* exhibition at the Royal Academy, 1930; they were then framed in a simpler moulding and laid flat in a shadow-box. The *altarino* has, however, been reconstructed on the basis of study of such surviving original Ducciesque triptychs as those in the National Gallery (566), the Museum of Fine Arts, Boston (45.880), in the Fogg Art Museum, Cambridge, Mass. (1922.108), and in the Pinacoteca in Siena (35).[1]

Shearman also provides a good account of the critical fortunes of the triptych since the time when Crowe and Cavalcaselle considered it 'second only in importance in Duccio's work to the *Maestà*'. As opposed to scholars who have accepted it as original, or as a product of Duccio's workshop, others, notably Stubblebine (1979) and White (1979), consider it to be the work of an independent follower. White acknowledges 'the general attractiveness of design and superb quality in the painting of heads and draperies' and the 'extreme virtuosity of the way in which

[1] We would wish to acknowledge the help which Professor John White gave in planning this reconstruction.

49 Central panel

the gold striations of the draperies are handled in order to create complex fold patterns'; but considers the striations and the limited range of tones unusual for Duccio. Above all, he finds unacceptable, at a late stage in the artist's career, the oddly constructed architectural elements in combination with so sophisticated a figure style. An unusual feature of the triptych was, originally, the quantity of blood displayed, dripping from Christ's elbows on to the rocks below. Much of it was removed by North, who considered it to have been put on in the nineteenth century; but there are still traces of it on Christ's body. Shearman thinks it 'inappropriate' to make such clear-cut statements about the smaller works with which the Duccio scholar has to concern himself and does not accept the 'assumption of consistency and logic' underlying White's views. He puts forward a date, *c.*1308–11, and considers, in relation to the iconography: 'it would be difficult to find a small Italian triptych of *c.*1310 as rich and logical in iconographic invention. A Franciscan patron seems virtually certain' (Shearman, No.86).

50

Gonzales Coques (*1614 or 1618–84*)

50 The Family of Jan-Baptista Anthoine
COLOUR PLATE XII (detail) between pages 80 and 81

Oil on copper: $22\frac{1}{4} \times 28\frac{15}{16}$ in., 56.5 × 73.5 cm. Signed and dated: *GONZALES.1664*. Bought by Seguier for George IV at the sale of Lord Radstock's pictures at Christie's, 13 May 1826 (29); formerly in the Gros, de Chalot and Helsleuter collections in Paris.

The family is identified by the coat of arms on the curtain. Jan-Baptista Anthoine (d.1687) was a knight and postmaster of Antwerp. He owned a good collection of pictures and, in an inventory drawn up in 1691, No.300 was 'Het portrait van de familie van Gonsael' (J. Denucé, *The Antwerp Art-Galleries* (Antwerp, 1932), p.364), which could be identified with No.50. Anthoine married Susanna Maria de Lannoy. They had two sons, Louis and Jan-Baptista, and two daughters, Maria-Alexandrina and Barbara Catharina.

No.50 is a very fine example of a family group which is not so much an early conversation-piece as an elaborate baroque group on a small scale. The Neptune fountain, the pergola supported by caryatids behind the father (derived from the background of Rubens's *Gerbier Family* in Washington) and the little dog, taken from Van Dyck, are stock accessories in Coques's repertory. The refined, liquid handling and delightful touches – the coral whistle, for example, clasped by the baby, and the hobbyhorse ridden by his older brother – are characteristic of Coques's work at this date. No.50 can be closely compared, for instance, in many of its details, with the *Family Group out of Doors* in the National Gallery. The appeal of such a work for connoisseurs in the time of George IV is well set out by Smith (*Catalogue Raisonné . . .* , part IV (1833), pp.257–8): 'However prolix this description may be, it conveys no idea of the superlative excellence of the work; nor is it possible to do it ample justice, by any lengthened detail of the various qualities which combine to make so perfect a work of art'.

51

Nicolaes Berchem (1620–83)

51 An Italian Landscape with Figures and Animals

Oil on panel: $13 \times 17\frac{3}{8}$ in., 33×44.1 cm. Signed and dated: *Berghem/1655*. Acquired by George IV with the Baring collection in 1814. Formerly in the Dufresne and de Bruijn collections in Amsterdam (sold respectively in 1770 and 1798).

A work in the artist's early mature manner. Christopher White (see below) lists the comparative material which supports the reading of the date as 1655 (Hofstede de Groot (1926) had read it as 1652); points out that No.51 'belongs to the group of broad river landscapes executed in the 1650s'; and suggests that the lighting, the landscapes and the buildings scattered therein, may reflect the impact of a visit to Italy, *c.*1653–5. Berchem was a prominent member of the second generation of Dutch Italianate painters. Always a very fine technician, a painter of immense facility, his work at this date is without the almost rococo flamboyance which it acquired later. In the eighteenth century Berchem was the best known of all the Dutch Italianate landscape painters; and it is easy to be reminded, by the crisp touch and clear tones in No.51, of the early work of Gainsborough. The riders and the dismounted figure would not lose their way in Cornard Wood (White, No.20).

52

53

Jan Brueghel (1568–1625)

52 A Flemish Fair

COLOUR PLATE IX (detail) facing page 64

Oil on copper: 18¾ × 27 in., 47.6 × 68.6 cm. Signed and dated: *BRVEGHEL A 1600*. Acquired, before July 1750, by Frederick, Prince of Wales, with a companion picture, *Adam and Eve in the Garden of Eden*. The pictures had probably been acquired in Spain by Sir Daniel Arthur. They were seen in the house of George Bagnall who had married Sir Daniel's widow. The *Fair* in particular is a reminder of the quality of the pictures acquired by the Prince of Wales: as important a work, although on so diminutive a scale, as the *Summer Landscape* by Rubens which he bought at about the same time.

Painted four years after the artist's return to Antwerp from Italy, the *Fair* still contains references to his father's work: in the peasant dance as well as in many of the gestures, expressions and tones. The main lines of the composition – a triangular plane marked out by a succession of groups of figures from the foreground into the middle distance on the left and a landscape stretching away to a far distance on the right – can be compared with the *Preaching of Christ* of 1598 in Munich (187), in which there is the same abundant anecdotal interest and rich variety of social class among the figures included in a crowded scene. Particularly characteristic of such works in Brueghel's *œuvre* is the group of well-dressed figures standing fairly near the foreground and slightly detached from the throng. In No.52 the father (?) of the family carries a sword, but his child appears, in a gesture which is developed later by Teniers, to be trying to make him take part in the dance. The recession back to the church, and the range of colours, are articulated by the patterns made by figures and groups and by a subtle play of contrasting light and shadow. In the other half of the composition the mountainous landscape, stretching away to an infinite distance and painted with exquisite delicacy in a range of blues, silvers and greys, is a striking example of Brueghel's '*Nah-Fern-Landschaft*' and of the miniature-like refinement with which he painted it. It is not surprising that the creator of such masterpieces was extremely successful and should, with Rubens, have dominated the artistic scene in Antwerp in the first quarter of the seventeenth century. When, for example, the Duke of Saxony came to Antwerp in 1614, he visited those two eminent painters. Brueghel, he wrote, painted little pictures with landscapes, but all so subtle and so artistic that one can only marvel at them (H. Gerson and E.H. Ter Kuile, *Art and Architecture in Belgium 1600 to 1800* (1960), p.58; *Between Renaissance and Baroque*, City of Manchester Art Gallery (1965), No.52; K. Ertz, *Jan Brueghel der Altere* (Cologne, 1979), pp.47–49, 567, No.60, and in *Bruegel Une dynastie de peintres*, op. cit., pp.165–76, No.121).

Adriaen van de Velde (1636–72)

53 Figures on the Coast at Scheveningen

Oil on canvas: 15⅛ × 19⅞ in., 38.4 × 50.5 cm. Signed and dated: *A.V.Velde.f./1660*. Acquired by George IV with the Baring collection in 1814. Formerly in the collection of the Countess of Holderness, daughter of Francis Doublet of Groeneveldt; sold at Christie's, 6 March 1802 (70).

Christopher White (see below) cites pictures related to No.53 in subject and date, notably the view of the beach in the Louvre (INV. 1915), painted in the same year. Van de Velde's rare beach scenes are his most original contribution to the development of Dutch landscape painting, with 'a freshness and a rarely matched plein-air effect' (J. Rosenberg, S. Slive and E.H. Ter Kuile, *Dutch Art and Architecture 1600 to 1800* (1966), p.161; and see especially W. Stechow, *Dutch Landscape Painting of the Seventeenth Century* (1968), pp.107–9). There are, in fact, only five such beach scenes in the artist's *œuvre*, all painted between 1658 and 1670. They are works of unusual charm, with their low horizons, quiet mood, broken sunshine, and unforced commentary on the social life of the seaside; and they make a striking contrast with the refinement of such works as No.37 (White, No.203; P.C. Sutton, *Masters of 17th-Century Dutch Landscape Painting*, Rijksmuseum, Amsterdam; Museum of Fine Arts, Boston; Philadelphia Museum of Art (1987–8), pp.493–5).

54

Cornelis van Poelenburch *(1586(?)–1667)*

54 Shepherds with their Flocks in a Landscape with Roman Ruins

Oil on copper: $12\frac{1}{2} \times 15\frac{3}{4}$ in., 31.7 × 40 cm. Signed: *C.P.* Acquired by George IV with the Baring collection in 1814; formerly in the Randon de Boisset collection in Paris (sold 1777).

Painted *c.*1620, some three years after Poelenburch, one of the first generation of Dutch Italianate landscape painters, had arrived in Rome. He was a founder member of the Roman *Schildersbent*. Exceptionally refined in quality, No.54 is a beautiful example of Poelenburch's imaginative attitude towards the remains of the classical past. It is a style much influenced by Bril and Elsheimer,

and very close to Breenbergh, but there is an individual quality in the light and the softened contours and in the tranquil mood created by groups of animals and figures near picturesque and semi-ruinous buildings, in this case the remains of the Temple of Castor and Pollux in the Forum. No.54 demonstrates the significance of Poelenburch's part in the development of the classical landscape and his influence even on so great an artist as Claude.

By 1625 Poelenburch had returned to Utrecht, his birthplace. Thereafter his work was as popular with royal and aristocratic patrons and collectors in Holland and England as it had been with distinguished connoisseurs in Italy (White, No.141).

55

Annibale Carracci (1560–1609)

55 Head of a Man in Profile

Oil on canvas: $17\frac{5}{8} \times 12\frac{5}{8}$ in., 44.8×32.1 cm. Recorded in the collection of George III and perhaps, as Sir Michael Levey has suggested, one of 'The heads two Carraccis by themselves' which Vertue noted in the collection of Frederick, Prince of Wales, in 1750.

This brilliantly painted and extraordinarily modern head is now generally accepted as by Annibale, c.1590, an example of his Venetian or neo-Venetian manner. There are, however, no certain portraits by him from this date with which it can be compared and no portraits in his *œuvre* as a whole which strike exactly this note (Levey, No.435; D. Posner, op. cit., vol.II, p.25; *Masters of the Loaded Brush*, Columbia University, New York (1967), No.1).

73

56

57

Richard Parkes Bonington (1802–28)

56 A Coast Scene in France
COLOUR PLATE XIV (detail) facing page 81

Oil on canvas: $18\frac{1}{8} \times 21\frac{3}{4}$ in., 46.4×55.2 cm. Signed and dated: *RP Bonington. 1826*. Originally in the collection of the 3rd Marquess of Lansdowne, a notable early collector of Bonington's work, who bought extensively at the sales held after the artist's death. Acquired from the Lansdowne collection in 1950 by the late Lord Plunket, Equerry to The Queen and Deputy Master of the Household. Always deeply and imaginatively interested in anything that concerned The Queen's collections and their display, Lord Plunket was involved from the beginning in establishing The Queen's Gallery. At the end of his life he had expressed a wish that The Queen should have his Bonington, a picture he especially loved; and after his death in 1975 it was given to her, in his memory, by his family.

Bonington had emigrated with his parents to Calais in 1817. He had sketched on the French coast and in the valley of the Seine since 1821 and frequently returned there. Marcia Pointon (see below) has pointed out that 'Bonington's views answered a demand for peaceful, picturesque views of the French coastline ... after years of threatened coastal invasion, warfare and civil unrest. They also provided a pictorial affirmation of the city-dweller's developing taste for sea air, boating and marine pleasures of all sorts.' No.56 is a particularly fine example of the painter's vision and of his ability to record simple scenes, on coasts and estuaries at low tide, in soft sunshine, peopled with fishermen and their families. Roger Fry considered that 'no English artist ever started his career with such an equipment as regards sheer manual dexterity and the instinct for discovering how to interpret his images in conformity with his technique'; and doubted if such gifts had been seen since the time of Rubens. Mrs Jameson, who saw the picture when it hung at Bowood, described it as 'Very fresh and beautiful in effect' (*Companion to the most celebrated Private Galleries of Art in London* (1844), p.322). There are obvious affinities between No.56 and the oil, *On the Coast of Picardy* in the Wallace Collection (P341), also painted in 1826; and a particularly splendid example of the type is the larger *Coast Scene* at Woburn. Most relevant for No.56, however, is the picture on the same scale, painted in the previous year, originally in the collection of Sir George Warrender and sold at Sotheby's, 14 March 1984

(82). In No.56 Bonington repeats the topographical background and, under the same early morning light, varies the disposition of the little children in the foreground, the basket of fish, the stones, the cart, the distant fisherman and the boat beached at low tide (M. Spencer, *R.P. Bonington*, Castle Museum and Art Gallery, Nottingham (1965), No.264; M. Pointon, *Bonington, Francia & Wyld* (1985); for Bonington, see particularly J. Ingamells, *Richard Parkes Bonington* (1979), and *The Wallace Collection Catalogue of Pictures*, I (1985), pp.19–74).

Pietro Longhi (1702–85)

57 The Morning Levee

Oil on panel: $19\frac{1}{4} \times 23\frac{3}{4}$ in., 48.9×60.3 cm. Signed and dated on the back: *Petrus Longhi/1744*. With its companion (No.67), acquired by George III with the collection of Consul Smith. The frames are good examples of the refined quality of those made in Venice for many of the Consul's pictures. At the time of the purchase there was apparently in his collection another pair of compositions by Longhi of the same, but horizontal, dimensions. Although almost certainly a pair, the iconographical link between the two subjects is not entirely clear; and it should be pointed out that, in the early list of pictures acquired from Smith, No.57 is described as: 'A Bride sitting by her Bridegroom in Bed'. The obviously tender look with which the rather elderly man in bed turns towards his young bride (?) may be an allusion to their union, which is happily less turbulent than that of Venus and Adonis in the two pictures hanging on either side of the bed.

Both pictures are fine examples, painted on an important commission, of Longhi's possibly rather over-rated talents: his anecdotal sense; his attention to such details as still-life and furnishings; the subtle humour and gaiety with which his scenes are so often charged; and his liking for pretty women and well-dressed young men. These qualities were admired by contemporaries. Pietro Guarienti, for instance, wrote in 1753 that Longhi had made an instant impression with his new and individual type of conversation piece, painted on a small scale and with such accuracy that people and places were instantly recognizable (the gentleman in No.57 is a particularly careful portrait); and G. Gozzi, eight years later, praised the artist for painting what he saw with his own eyes (instead of loftier themes) and for creating in his small scenes an atmosphere of good humour (both quoted by Spike, see below). There are five preparatory drawings for No.57 in the Museo Correr (Levey, No.537; T. Pignatti, *Pietro Longhi* (Venice, 1968), p.117; ibid., *L'opera completa di Pietro Longhi* (Milan, 1974), No.38; J.T. Spike, *Giuseppe Maria Crespi and the Emergence of Genre Painting in Italy*, Kimbell Art Museum, Fort Worth (1986), p.189, No.41).

Marco Ricci (1676–1730)

58 A Ruin Caprice

Tempera on leather: 13 × 18 in., 33 × 45.7 cm. Nos.58–65 are a selection from the set of thirty-two landscapes in this medium by Marco Ricci which were in the collection of Consul Smith. An inscription, *Per Madama Smit*, on the back of one in the series (Levey, No.598), indicates that it was perhaps a present from the artist; and as it is closely related to a drawing, signed and dated 27 July 1710, the related painting in tempera may have been the first work by the artist to enter Smith's collection, which was to become outstandingly rich in works by Marco Ricci and his uncle, Sebastiano. The group of landscapes in tempera (the leather on which they are painted is chamois) was probably assembled over a number of years by Smith; one of them is dated 1728. Hanging together, in their pretty contemporary Venetian frames and bevilled glasses, the series would have made a ravishing impression in a little room in Smith's villa or small *palazzo*. In the time of George III they hung, it seems, in the Queen's Dressing-Room at Kew. Six of the set were included by Fossati in his publication (Venice, 1743) of works by Marco Ricci in Smith's collection. Two are closely connected with etchings by Ricci himself.

Landscapes in tempera played an increasing part in Marco Ricci's *œuvre* from *c.*1720 onwards. In these brilliant but fragile little works the full range of Ricci's invention, as Sir Michael Levey has demonstrated, is displayed. The treatment of landscape is varied, spacious and, in a quiet way, often exciting. There are reminiscences of early Venetian approaches to landscape, and of such Italianate Dutch artists as Berchem. The imaginative treatment of the pleasure of ruins recalls such painters as Poelenburch and is of obvious significance for Canaletto, and Piranesi, among others. Particularly enchanting are the pictures of informal domestic scenes such as No.59 below (Levey, p.34 (for the series), No.604; useful material also in G.M. Pilo, *Marco Ricci*, Bassano del Grappa – Palazzo Sturm (1963), especially pp.95–120).

59 The Courtyard of a Country House

Tempera on leather: 12¼ × 18 in., 31.1 × 45.7 cm (Levey, No.593; *Venetian Baroque and Rococo*, Ferens Art Gallery, Hull (1967), No.56).

60 A Woodland Scene with Bandits

COLOUR PLATE XI (detail) facing page 80

Tempera on leather: 12 × 18 in., 30.5 × 45.7 cm. There is a closely related drawing at Windsor; and the composition is among those engraved by Fossati (see above) (Levey, No.613).

61 A Woodland Scene with a Bear frightening Peasants

Tempera on leather: 12⅝ × 18 in., 32.1 × 45.7 cm (Levey, No.591).

62 A Landscape with two Monks in Prayer

Tempera on leather: 12¼ × 17¾ in., 31.1 × 45.1 cm. There is a closely related drawing by Ricci at Windsor; and he etched a version of the composition, in reverse and with slight variations. The composition was engraved in 1730 by Carlo Orsolini (Levey, No.614).

63 A rocky Landscape with Hermits

Tempera on leather: 11¼ × 17¾ in., 28.6 × 44.1 cm (Levey, No.600).

58

61

59

62

60

63

64

65

Marco Ricci (1676–1730)

64 A Landscape with Herds watering

Tempera on leather: $12\frac{1}{2} \times 17\frac{7}{8}$ in., 31.8×45.4 cm (Levey, No.594).

65 A Ruin Caprice

Tempera on leather: $13\frac{1}{4} \times 18$ in., 33.7×45.7 cm. Engraved by Fossati (see above). The composition was a favourite one in Marco Ricci's *œuvre* and a number of versions exist. Its grandeur and sense of romance, and some of Ricci's exciting compositional devices in designing such a work, can be found in his large oil paintings (e.g., G.M. Pilo, op. cit., Nos.60–64) (Levey, No.597).

Rosalba Carriera (1675–1757)

66 Portrait of the Artist

Pastel on paper: $22\frac{1}{2} \times 18\frac{1}{2}$ in., 57.2×47 cm. The artist was born, and died, in Venice, where she was famous as a portraitist in pastel, patronized particularly by English and French visitors to the city and by patrons in France and Germany. In the use of her chosen medium, in colour, skill at getting a likeness and virtuosity of touch, she was unsurpassed. This, probably the last of her numerous self-portraits, she gave to Joseph Smith after he became Consul (1744) but before c.1746, when she went blind. Smith owned a considerable group of works by her. They presumably were among the works acquired with Smith's collection by George III, but only six, including No.66, survive in the collection today. This likeness of the artist in old age closely resembles her image of herself as the Muse of Tragedy (Sir M. Levey, *Painting in XVIII Century Venice* (1959), pp.141–3; Levey, No.446).

66

67

Pietro Longhi (1702–85)

67 Blind Man's Buff

Oil on panel: 19 × 23 in., 48.3 × 58.4 cm. Signed and dated: *Petrus Longhi F. 174[ ]*; the last digit is indecipherable. See No.57, to which it was presumably painted as a pair. Spike (loc. cit.) has pointed out that in a pair of pictures in Washington, *The Swoon* and *The Game of Pentola*, painted in the same year, Longhi made the same association between a boudoir scene and a game.

The large picture in the background appears to show a queen (?) with a group of attendant figures. There is a drawing in the Museo Correr for the stool and various legs (Levey, No.538; T. Pignatti, op. cit., p.117; ibid., *L'opera completa di Pietro Longhi* (Milan, 1974), No.38).

68

Sir David Wilkie (1785–1841)

68 The Defence of Saragossa

Oil on canvas: $37 \times 55\frac{1}{2}$ in., 94×141 cm. Signed and dated: *David Wilkie. Madrid 1828*. Wilkie had arrived in Madrid on 9 October 1827 and left on 2 April 1828. He brought back to London the three pictures which he had painted of scenes from the Spanish guerrilla struggle against Napoleon's troops. They were all exhibited at the Royal Academy in 1829 (*The Defence of Saragossa* was No.128). Wilkie was summoned to St James's to show George IV the pictures he had painted abroad. The King acquired the three Spanish pictures and commissioned Wilkie to paint a fourth to complete the series.

The King had always been a generous patron of Wilkie and was now clearly excited by the fresh colour and fluent handling of Wilkie's Italian and Spanish subjects in which the influence of Rubens partly modifies Wilkie's debt to Velázquez and Murillo. Wilkie's receipt for 2,000 guineas for his three Spanish pictures is dated 19 March 1829. Francis Collins's bill (£36. 11s.) for the frames had been submitted in January.

The defence of Saragossa, in the summer of 1808, was one of the most celebrated events in the Spanish insurrection against the French, who had appeared before the city on 15 June but were compelled to raise the siege early in August. During the siege a heavy attack had been launched (on 2 July) on the west and south sides of the city. General Palafox, the famous guerrilla leader, was with a small battery at the Convent of Sta Engracia near the Portillo Gate. The gunners had been shot down and, as one lay dying, his wife, Agostina Zaragoza, seized the

PLATE XI
Detail from *A Woodland Scene with Bandits*
by Marco Ricci (No.60)

The following pages:

PLATE XII
Detail from *The Family of Jan-Baptista Anthoine*
by Gonzales Coques (No.50)

PLATE XIII
Detail from *Le Tambour Battant*
by David Teniers the Younger (No.48)

lighted match from his hand and fired the gun at point-blank range into the French column. The attack was repulsed and Palafox, on the spot, gave Agostina a commission as sub-lieutenant of artillery. Wilkie described his picture in the catalogue entry for the Royal Academy in 1829: the gun is being trained by Palafox and Father Consolaçion, an Augustinian friar; behind the gun is the priest Boggiero, Palafox's tutor and another hero of the resistance, writing a dispatch. Wilkie himself said earlier of the picture that it was 'capable of a striking and uncommon effect both of composition and colour'; and the dramatic action is matched by a fluency of touch and purity of tone which Wilkie seldom surpassed. He had begun the picture by 17 March 1828; a preliminary sketch in watercolour, in which all the principal elements of the composition have been established, is signed and dated 29 November 1827. General Palafox had been introduced into the composition at the advice of Prince Dolgoruki, who was attached to the Russian Legation at Madrid and to whom Wilkie wrote of their mutual admiration of Titian. Wilkie's style had been dramatically transformed, by illness, travel and fresh visual excitements, from the tighter and more delicate manner with which the public had hitherto associated him. He himself described the 'change, and they say for the better, in the colouring and larger style of execution' noted by those who saw his pictures before the Academy exhibition of 1829 was opened. The change, however, was by no means universally admired; and the King's purchase of no less than five of the pictures was an act of conspicuous generosity and enthusiasm, a notable gesture of support for the painter at a crucial moment in his career. When the King died, Wilkie described him as 'the greatest friend I have ever met with'.

The courage of the Maid became a legend. Byron saw her in Seville in 1809 and celebrated her heroism at Saragossa in the first canto of *Childe Harold's Pilgrimage*. She was firmly established in 'the company of other heroines of revolutionary legend' (Millar, No.1180; R.D. Altick, *Painting from Books . . . 1760–1900* (Columbus, 1985), p.438; H.A.D. Miles and D.B. Brown, *Sir David Wilkie of Scotland (1785–1841)*, North Carolina Museum of Art, Raleigh (1987), p.34, No.30).

PLATE XIV
Detail from *A Coast Scene in France*
by Richard Parkes Bonington (No.56)

69

John Hoppner (1758(?)–1810)

69 Joseph Haydn (1732–1809)

Oil on canvas: $36\frac{1}{4} \times 28\frac{1}{4}$ in., 92.1 × 71.7 cm. The composer paid two highly successful visits to London and on both occasions was brought into contact with the royal family. In January 1791 he was presented at a court ball at St James's and attended a chamber concert at Carlton House. In the autumn he stayed with the Duke and Duchess of York at Oatlands and conducted his music. 'The Prince of Wales sat on my right side and played with us on his violincello, quite tolerably . . . he has an extraordinary love of music and a lot of feeling, but not much money.' In 1792 Haydn went to Ascot for the royal meeting. On the second visit, 1794–5, he conducted his own works, was presented by the Prince to the King and Queen and played at twenty-six concerts at Carlton House.

It was during the first visit that the Prince of Wales commissioned Hoppner to paint Haydn's portrait. Hoppner was at work on it in December 1791. Haydn was an exemplary sitter, very anxious that he should be seen – and recorded – at his best. The portrait was not finished when Haydn, on 23 June 1792, left England, but it was described (in the *Quarterly Review*, October 1817) as 'so striking a likeness of this extraordinary man, that the Prince of Wales . . . would not permit Hoppner to touch it after his departure'. It remains a vivid demonstration of Hoppner's sympathetic characterization and, since recent cleaning and restoration, an illustration of his essentially superficial technique. The account in the *Quarterly Review* may be apocryphal. The portrait, for which the Prince paid £31. 10s., was among pictures delivered to Carlton House after Hoppner's death by his widow (Millar, No.843; *Joseph Haydn in seiner Zeit*, Eisenstadt (1982), No.604).

Miniatures

70

71

Hans Holbein the Younger (1497/8–1543)

70 Charles Brandon, 3rd Duke of Suffolk (1537/8–51)

Watercolour on vellum: circular, 2¼ in., 5.7 cm. Inscribed: *ANN/1541/.ETATIS SVÆ 3/.10.MARCI.* The portraits of the two Brandon boys were given to Charles I by Sir Henry Fanshawe. The frame of one of them was described at the time as 'a round double turnd ivorie Box without anie Christalls'. The King's collection of miniatures, which numbered nearly eighty, was kept in cupboards in the Cabinet Room at Whitehall (QG, 1978–9, No.86; J. Murdoch and others, *The English Miniature* (1981), pp.36–7; Strong, *Tudor Court*, No.35; Strong, 1983, p.50; J. Rowlands, op. cit., pp.151–2, M.11).

Hans Holbein the Younger (1497/8–1543)

71 Henry Brandon, 2nd Duke of Suffolk (1535–51)

Watercolour on vellum: circular, 2¼ in., 5.7 cm. Inscribed: *ETATIS. SVÆ.5.6. SEPDEM./ANNO/1535.* The two boys were sons of Charles Brandon, 1st Duke of Suffolk (d.1545), and his fourth wife, Catherine. The elder boy was educated with the young Prince Edward and carried the Orb at his Coronation. On that occasion both boys were made Knights of the Bath. They were both at St John's College, Cambridge, and were renowned for their learning. Their untimely death of sweating sickness in 1551, within half an hour of each other, deeply impressed their contemporaries, one of whom described the older boy as '*animosus, fortis, robustus, et ad militarem disciplinam, non factus, sed natus*'; his brother as '*non robustus . . . sed elegans*' (QG, 1978–9, No.85; J. Murdoch, loc. cit.; Strong, *Tudor Court*, No.34; Strong, 1983, p.50; J. Rowlands, op. cit., p.151, M.10).

Nos.70 and 71 belong to the small group of portrait miniatures painted by Holbein at the court of Henry VIII: immeasurably more accomplished than the miniatures produced earlier in the King's reign, normally associated with Lucas Horenbout (or Hornebolte) and painted in a distinctively Flemish style. More modern in feeling and closer to Holbein's style as a painter of miniatures are the portraits, the *Preux de Marignan*, painted by Jean Clouet in a manuscript made for Francis

I, 1518–19, *Les Commentaires de la Guerre Gallique*. The circular form, lucid presentation and brilliant blue bice backgrounds, so characteristic of Holbein's miniatures, are all to be found in Clouet's miniatures. They are painted in the same technique; they have the broad gold border which Holbein uses in Nos.70 and 71; and there is in Clouet's method of producing an image the same close association, as there is in Holbein's, between a portrait drawing and a miniature (P. Mellen, *Jean Clouet* (1971), pp.37–42). Clouet's *Preux de Marignan* can probably be regarded as the earliest examples in the history of the portrait miniature as an independent art form; but compared with them Holbein's work in miniature is more subtle and varied in mood and richer in treatment of the surface. He was also more successful in creating a fully three-dimensional image. The circular form of Clouet's and Holbein's miniatures emphasizes the significance of the portrait medal in the genesis of the miniature. Technical examination (1977) of Nos.70 and 71 revealed that the hands in both had been corrected by the artist himself.

72

Hans Holbein the Younger (1497/8–1543)

72 Elizabeth, Lady Audley

Watercolour on vellum: circular, $2\frac{1}{2}$ in., 6.4 cm. Conceivably in the later Stuart collection, but more probably acquired by Queen Victoria; and recorded in a list, drawn up in 1870, of miniatures in the Royal Library. The portrait is very closely related to a drawing by

Holbein in the Royal Collection; both are dated *c*.1540. The sitter is thought to be Elizabeth, daughter of the Marquis of Dorset, who married in 1538 Thomas, Lord Audley of Walden. After his death in 1544 his widow married (1549) Sir George Norton (QG, 1978–9, No.84; J. Murdoch, op. cit., p.37; Strong, *Tudor Court*, No.31; Strong, 1983, p.47; J. Rowlands, op. cit., p.151, M.9).

73

Hans Holbein the Younger (1497/8–1543)

73 Portrait of a Lady

Watercolour on vellum: circular, $2\frac{1}{2}$ in., 6.4 cm. Almost certainly acquired by Queen Victoria and, from the early 1840s, considered to be a portrait of Catherine Howard. There is, in fact, no certain likeness of her with which No.73 can be compared; but most writers have noted the similarity between No.73 and a female portrait, perhaps of a member of the Cromwell family, in Toledo (J. Rowlands, op. cit., p.146, No.69). Recently (see Strong, *Tudor Court*) arguments have been put forward in favour of the traditional identification. Comparison with a portrait painted on the scale of life illustrates Holbein's genius in compressing into so tiny a compass his full renaissance sense of volume and movement and a notable feeling for character. Probably painted *c*.1540. Another version is in the collection of the Duke of Buccleuch. Of the two versions, No.73 is perhaps the one painted *ad vivum* (QG, 1978–9, No.84; Strong, *Tudor Court*, No.33; Strong, 1983, p.47; J. Rowlands, op. cit., p.151, M.8).

74

75

Jean Clouet (c.1485–90(?)–1540/1)

74 Francis, Dauphin of France (1518–36)

Watercolour on vellum: circular, $2\frac{3}{8}$ in., 6 cm. Probably acquired by Queen Victoria after 1881. The sitter was the eldest son of Francis I.

The portrait is close in style to those of the *Preux de Marignan* by Jean Clouet (see above); but was probably produced *c.*1525–8, slightly later than Clouet's drawing of the Dauphin in the Musée Condé and the related oil painting in Antwerp. It is therefore an important example of the type of miniature which may have influenced Holbein and which demonstrates the essential link, in Clouet's method, between the drawn, limned and painted images, as well as Clouet's importance in the evolution of the miniature portrait in the round. No.74 is, in Graham Reynolds's words, 'the earliest known example by Jean Clouet of a miniature fully on its own'. Strong and Reynolds draw attention to the lockets, sent to Henry VIII in 1526 by Francis I's sister, Madame d'Alençon, containing miniatures, which may well have been by Clouet, of the King and his two sons, the Dauphin and his younger brother: a very early instance of the use of miniatures as presents, painted for a special purpose and charged with meaning of various kinds, between the courts of Europe. In 1526 the two boys were being held as hostages in Spain after their father's defeat at Pavia in the previous year; and Henry VIII was being asked to help in securing their release. The lockets made a considerable impression at the English court (P. Mellen, op. cit., p.234, No.135; Strong, *Tudor Court*, No.4; Strong, 1983, pp.27–9; unpublished notes by Graham Reynolds).

Isaac Oliver (c.1565–1617)

75 Portrait of the Artist

Watercolour on vellum: oval, $1\frac{3}{4} \times 1\frac{1}{2}$ in., 4.4 × 3.8 cm. Signed in monogram: *IO*. Acquired by Frederick, Prince of Wales; formerly in the collection of Dr Richard Mead. Probably painted *c.*1590–5, when the artist was aged about thirty. His father, a Huguenot goldsmith from Rouen, had settled in London with his family in 1568. Discussing this miniature, and the *Self-portrait* in the National Portrait Gallery of about the same date, Horace Walpole made his well-known remark: 'The art of the master and the imitator of nature are so great in it that the largest magnifying-glass only calls out new beauties' (*Anecdotes of Painting*, ed. J. Dalloway and R.N. Wornum (1888), vol.I, p.178); and, even at this early date in his career, and on so minute a scale, Oliver displays complete self-confidence and maturity as an artist: inventive in pose, realistic and, in this instance, witty, almost rakish in presentation, and using a strong chiaroscuro in modelling the flesh which, with his assured draughtsmanship, produces an impression very different from that created by Hilliard. In mood, and to some extent in composition, the portrait is close to Oliver's earliest dated miniature, the portrait of a lady (1587) in the Buccleuch collection (J. Finsten, *Isaac Oliver Art at the Courts of Elizabeth I and James I* (1981), vol.II, pp.32–3, Cat.18; Strong, *Tudor Court*, No.134; J. Murrell, *The Way Howe to Lymne* (1983), p.39).

76

of the melancholy mood. Finsten (loc. cit.) points out the likeness, in the broadest terms, between Oliver's composition and the title-page of Robert Burton's 1628 edition of *The Anatomy of Melancholy*. The architectural background to the garden, useful evidence of the appearance of a grand late Tudor lay-out, is adapted from an architectural fantasy in the *Artis Perspectivae . . .* (1568) by Jan Vredeman de Vries (J. Murdoch, op. cit., pp.70–71; J. Finsten, op. cit., vol.I, pp.100–3, vol.II, pp.18–22, Cat.13; R. Strong, *The Renaissance Garden in England* (1979), p.70; Strong, *Tudor Court*, No.268; Strong, 1983, pp.154–5; J. Murrell, op. cit., p.40; M. Edmond, *Hilliard and Oliver* (1983), pp.111–12).

77

Isaac Oliver *(c.1565–1617)*

76 Portrait of a young Man

Watercolour on vellum: $5 \times 3\frac{1}{2}$ in., 12.7×8.9 cm. Signed in monogram: *IO*. Acquired by Frederick, Prince of Wales; formerly in the collection of Dr Richard Mead. At that time, and for many years thereafter, stated to be a portrait of Sir Philip Sidney. No.76 can be dated, on the costume alone, to *c*.1590.

One of the most celebrated portraits of the Tudor period and an early example, in the history of British painting, of the full-length in a landscape; it is also the first portrait by Oliver on this scale, earlier and slightly larger than the biggest of Hilliard's full-length miniatures and painted in a more realistic and fundamentally Netherlandish style. The sitter's folded arms, and details in his costume, probably indicate that the portrait is partly an illustration

Isaac Oliver *(c.1565–1617)*

77 Portrait of a young Woman

Watercolour on vellum: oval, $3 \times 2\frac{1}{4}$ in., 7.6×5.7 cm. Acquired by Frederick, Prince of Wales; formerly in the collection of Dr Richard Mead. At the time of its purchase considered to be a portrait of Mary, Queen of Scots: 'an admirable piece', in Horace Walpole's words, 'though very doubtful whether of her'.

Probably painted *c*.1595. So far from being the tragic Queen of Scots, the sitter was presumably the wife of a rich citizen of London. The scale of the portrait is significantly larger than the standard format for an oval head and shoulders limning; and the ultramarine used in the background was an expensive pigment. The portrait is in exceptionally good condition and a technical *tour de force*, modelled with extreme refinement to create a fully rounded, richly shadowed illusion of the sitter's presence. A plumbago drawing after No.77, but in reverse, by Thomas Worlidge, signed and dated 1737, was sold at Christie's, 12 December 1978 (27) (J. Finsten, op. cit., vol.I, pp.112–13, vol.II, pp.63–5, Cat.38; Strong, *Tudor Court*, No.160; Strong, 1983, p.166; M. Edmond, op. cit., p.111).

miniatures he produced of and for his patron, No.78, probably painted *c*.1612, is the most important, as well as the largest. It was repeated in Oliver's *atelier* on a smaller scale, with variations, and became the accepted image of the Prince. When, for example, posthumous portraits were required in the time of Charles I, it was this likeness which painters such as Mytens and Van Dyck were required to use. As a limned portrait No.78 is on a bigger scale than anything produced earlier; and it anticipates in scale and design the large miniatures produced by John Hoskins some twenty years later of Charles I, Henrietta Maria and, for example, Lady Dysart (Ham House). On so large a scale the art of the miniaturist, as practised at that date, was taxed to its limits to convey so rounded an image. A small *trompe l'œil* effect is produced by allowing the Garter badge to fall over the feigned border at the bottom. The presentation of the sitter in this martial context could be linked in the imagination with the roles in which he was cast by Inigo Jones and Ben Jonson in the *Barriers* (1610) and the *Masque of Oberon* (1611), and with the many tributes to his delight in the military arts (J. Finsten, op. cit., vol.II, pp.98–100, Cat.63; Strong, *Tudor Court*, No.257; Strong, 1983, pp.171–3; J. Murrell, op. cit., pp.45–46; M. Edmond, op. cit., pp.152–4; Sir R. Strong, *Henry, Prince of Wales* (1986), pp.119, 179).

78

79

Isaac Oliver (c.1565–1617)

78 Henry, Prince of Wales (1594–1612)

Watercolour on vellum: $5\frac{1}{8} \times 4$ in., 13×10.2 cm. Recorded in the collection of Charles I as: 'the biggest lim'd Picture that was made by Prince Henry being lim'd in a sett laced Roofe in a gilded Armor ...'. Isaac Oliver was in Prince Henry's service at least from early in 1609. Of the

Isaac Oliver (c.1565–1617)

79 John Donne (1573–1631)

Watercolour on vellum: oval, $1\frac{3}{4} \times 1\frac{7}{16}$ in., 4.4×3.7 cm. Signed and dated: *.1616*. *IO* (initials in monogram). Purchased for the Royal Collection at the Sackville Bale sale, Christie's, 24 May 1881 (1426); formerly in the collection of Lord Northwick.

Painted in the year after the poet had been ordained. He was Chaplain in Ordinary to James I and Divinity Reader at Lincoln's Inn. In 1621 he was appointed Dean of St Paul's. Although one of the artist's latest works, it is painted, as J. Murrell pointed out (see below) in a rather old-fashioned style. It was probably the source of the engraving by Merian for the title-page of Donne's *Sermons* (published in 1640), many of which he had delivered before James I and Charles I (J. Finsten, op. cit., vol.I, p.134, vol.II, pp.124–5, Cat.81; Strong, *Tudor Court*, No.178; Strong, 1983, p.180; J. Murrell, op. cit., pp.41, 44).

brother (No.78) to whom the Princess was devoted (J. Finsten, op. cit., vol.I, pp.130–1, vol.II, pp.85–6, Cat.53; Strong, *Tudor Court*, No.262; M. Edmond, op. cit., p.171).

81

John Hoskins (c.1590–1665)

81 Portrait of a Man

Watercolour on vellum: oval, $2\frac{3}{8} \times 1\frac{7}{8}$ in., 6×4.8 cm. Signed in monogram: *IH*. Acquired by Queen Victoria, and recorded in a list of her miniatures, drawn up in 1852, as a portrait of the 2nd Viscount Falkland. Probably painted c.1620.

80

Isaac Oliver (c.1565–1617)

80 Princess Elizabeth (1596–1662), later Queen of Bohemia

Watercolour on vellum: oval, $2 \times 1\frac{5}{8}$ in., 5.1×4.1 cm. Signed in monogram: *IO*. Oliver had been appointed in June 1605 'Painter for the Art of limning' to Queen Anne of Denmark with an annual salary of forty pounds. No.80, which had probably been painted for the Queen, was recorded in the collection of Charles I: 'Don . . . by the life . . . upon an Ovall blew grounded Card the Picture of your Ma^ts Sister when she was younger in her high time past fashioned haire dressing adorn'd at her head wth some single Elengtine Roases wth Carnation and white Ribbons in a white Ivory Box with a Christall over it'. She married the King of Bohemia in 1613.

Painted from life (see above), No.80 is one of the liveliest of Oliver's royal portraits: close in mood to his unfinished miniature of Charles I, when Prince of Wales, and, on its small scale, as finely wrought as the great miniature of the

82

John Hoskins (c.1590–1665)

82 Portrait of a Woman

Watercolour on vellum: oval, $2 \times 1\frac{5}{8}$ in., 5.1×4.1 cm. Signed: *IH*. Recorded in the collection of Queen Victoria, in the early part of her reign, as a portrait of the wife of Oliver Cromwell. Probably painted *c*.1645.

The controversy surrounding the work of John Hoskins, and the extent and quality of work which may have been done in his studio by his son, as well as the arguments prompted by the striking differences in technique and presentation – the lack of an ordered chronological artistic development – between miniatures signed by Hoskins, differences which can be linked perhaps with the varied form the signature can take, have been well summarized by John Murdoch (see below). No.81, which can be safely attributed to John Hoskins *père*, is painted in an old-fashioned style, less robust and more obviously English than the works of Isaac or Peter Oliver. No.82 is probably by the same hand, but the more naturalistic treatment of the figure and the three-dimensional image are notably more modern, revealing something of the influence of Van Dyck to which both Hoskins and his nephew, Samuel Cooper, reacted. It has been suggested that the sitter may be the artist's first wife (Foskett, N.P.G., No.153; J. Murdoch, 'Hoskins' and Crosses: Work in Progress', *Burl. Mag.*, vol.CXX (1978), pp.284–8, and op. cit., pp.95–104).

83

Samuel Cooper (1608(?)–72)

83 Portrait of the Artist (?)

Watercolour on vellum: oval, $2\frac{7}{8} \times 2\frac{1}{4}$ in., 7.3×5.7 cm. Signed and dated: *S : Cooper/fe : 1645*; and incised on the back: *Samuel Cooper/fecit feberuaris/1644/ould stile*. Seen by Vertue at Kensington in 1734: 'a high finishd limning being Cooper the limner. S. Cooper.f.1645. his own picture'; continued to be described as a self-portrait until at least 1862; but by 1881 identified as a portrait of Robert Walker, the painter, on the basis of his self-portrait at Hampton Court (Millar, No.207). There is, however, conspicuously little resemblance between the two portraits, except that in both the sitter looks over his right shoulder; and the old identification with the artist himself should be reconsidered.

One of the artist's finest portraits, unsurpassed in his *œuvre* and in the history of the miniature in England for the brilliance with which the sitter's physical presence is conjured up: an impression created partly by the soft greyish tonality, and by such details as the slightly parted lips and the modelling of the collar. It is probably the first English miniature in which the sitter looks out over his shoulder, a dramatic baroque device which Cooper derived partly from his knowledge of Van Dyck but (perhaps) also partly from Dutch sources, such as the figure of Bartolomeus Spranger in the younger Sadeler's engraving (1600) of Spranger with an allegory of the death of his wife (Foskett, N.P.G., No.11 and pp.XVI–XVII).

84

Samuel Cooper (1608(?)–72)

84 Catherine of Braganza (1638–1705)

Watercolour on vellum: oval, $4\frac{7}{8} \times 3\frac{7}{8}$ in., 12.4 × 9.8 cm. The five large unfinished portraits by Cooper, painted *c*.1663–4, are unique in his *œuvre*: described by John Murdoch (see below) as 'his most inventive and surprising contribution to the national iconography'. Unfinished miniatures by Cooper are not uncommon. Three, for example, are contained in the Pocket-Book in the Victoria and Albert Museum (G. Reynolds, *Samuel Cooper's Pocket-Book* (1975)), but they are on the normal miniature scale. Cooper also produced a number of large miniatures in which the size of the heads approximates to that in the five in The Queen's collection. Such large miniatures are always of very grand sitters: the King, the Earls of Shaftesbury and Arlington and the Grand Duke of Tuscany (Foskett, N.P.G., Nos.111, 112, 127, 128; ibid., *Samuel Cooper* (1974), Pl.74). If the miniatures of Shaftesbury, the King and the Grand Duke had been taken no further than Nos.84–8, they would have made

the same impression; the miniature of Arlington, left unfinished, was probably completed by a less skilful hand.

Nos.84–8 were among the miniatures ('*alcuni finiti solo nella testa*') which the Grand Duke, who had himself sat to Cooper in London in 1669, knew to be in the possession of the artist's widow in February 1677 and which he was inclined to acquire. He did not, in fact, do so and by 1706 they had entered the Royal Collection. Queen Caroline had them hanging in her Closet at Kensington by 1728. They were then in black oval frames so they had probably already been reduced to their present proportions and made, thereby, into a series uniform in size. The portraits had probably been executed originally on rectangular sheets of vellum *c*.$8\frac{1}{4} \times 6\frac{5}{8}$ in., 21 × 16.8 cm. It is significant that a copy by Mrs Rosse of No.88 is on a rectangular sheet, $8\frac{1}{2} \times 6\frac{3}{4}$ in., 21.6 × 17.1 cm (Reynolds, op. cit., p.2); and that when the Grand Duke was considering the purchase of works from Mrs Cooper he should have described at least two of them as of the same size as his own portrait by Cooper (i.e., $8\frac{1}{4} \times 6\frac{5}{8}$ in., 21 × 16.8 cm) and should have remembered the unfinished portraits as '*fino al ginocchio*'.

It is sometimes stated that the unfinished portraits had been kept by Cooper so that he could produce miniatures from them without renewed recourse to the sitters. They are among the most discerning and beautiful English portraits of the Stuart period, unsurpassed as much for their humanity and understanding as for their broad modelling and fluent handling. The heads have clearly been painted *ad vivum*. The hair is not always entirely finished. The dress is only lightly indicated. Only in No.87 is the background finished. In Nos.86 and 88 there is only a swift indication of the colour which is to be developed around the sitter's head and shoulders. A wash of opaque white is applied over the unfinished areas.

Daughter of John IV, King of Portugal. Married to Charles II, 21 May 1662. The marriage proved childless. Small, dark-skinned and shy, the Queen was humiliated by the King's absorption in a succession of beautiful and vivacious women who bore him many children (Foskett, N.P.G., No.79; J. Murdoch, op. cit., pp.116–20).

85

86

Samuel Cooper (1608(?)–72)

85 Frances Stuart, Duchess of Richmond (1648–1702)

Watercolour on vellum: oval, $4\frac{7}{8} \times 3\frac{7}{8}$ in., 12.4 × 9.8 cm. See No.84. The portraits of '*Madama la Duchessa di Richemont, quand'era giovanetta*', and of Albemarle (No.87), had stayed in the Grand Duke's memory as '*condotti con molto spirito, e felicità, se bene il primo non era ancora compito*'. In the list of available miniatures, No.85 was said to show the sitter at the age of sixteen or seventeen. A copy on a reduced scale is at Badminton.

Daughter of Walter Stuart of Blantyre; Maid of Honour and (1668) Lady of the Bedchamber to the Queen; and one of the most celebrated beauties of the Restoration court. Charles II was besotted by her and furious when she married secretly, in 1667, the 3rd Duke of Richmond. When Pepys visited Cooper's house on 30 March 1668, he saw 'Mrs. Stewards picture as when a young maid', before she had been a victim of smallpox, and was greatly moved by the difference in her appearance (Foskett, N.P.G., No.82).

Samuel Cooper (1608(?)–72)

86 Barbara Villiers, Duchess of Cleveland (c.1641–1709)

Watercolour on vellum: oval, $4\frac{7}{8} \times 3\frac{7}{8}$ in., 12.4 × 9.8 cm. See No.84. The sitter's countenance is close to that in a small finished miniature by Cooper, painted in 1661, in the Royal Collection.

Daughter of William Villiers, 2nd Viscount Grandison. Married (1659) to the Earl of Castlemaine, she had earlier been through a passionate affair with Lord Chesterfield. She first met the King in The Hague in 1659 and at the Restoration was soon established as the King's mistress, as rapacious and promiscuous as she was beautiful: 'the finest woman of her age'. She bore the King six (?) children and – a particularly callous action – was installed by him in 1662 as a Lady of the Bedchamber to the Queen (Foskett, N.P.G., No.81).

87

88

Samuel Cooper (1608(?)–72)

Samuel Cooper (1608(?)–72)

87 George Monck, 1st Duke of Albemarle (1608–70)

Watercolour on vellum: oval, $4\frac{7}{8} \times 3\frac{7}{8}$ in., 12.4×9.8 cm. See No.84. When Pepys visited Cooper's house on 30 March 1668, 'my Lord Generalls' was among the portraits he saw. Cooper's image was used in the production of a number of portraits of Monck on the scale of life; and a signed miniature of this type by Cooper himself is in the Buccleuch collection. In these he is seen in armour with the ribbon of the Garter (Foskett, N.P.G., No.91).

A professional soldier who had been 'very firm to Cromwell' and commander-in-chief of the Parliament forces in Scotland, he played a crucial part in bringing about the Restoration: 'engaged in conscience and honour to see my country freed from that intolerable slavery of a sword government'. He was rewarded with high office, a dukedom and the Garter (Foskett, N.P.G., No.80; L. Stainton and C. White, *Drawing in England from Hilliard to Hogarth* (British Museum and the Yale Center for British Art, New Haven, 1987), No.113).

88 James, Duke of Monmouth (1649–85)

Watercolour on vellum: oval, $4\frac{7}{8} \times 3\frac{7}{8}$ in., 12.4×9.8 cm. See No.84. In the list of miniatures possibly available for purchase by the Grand Duke, the unfinished head of Monmouth was said to show him at the age of fifteen. The King's son by Lucy Walters (or Barlow), he had been born in Rotterdam, educated in Paris and brought to London in the summer of 1662. 'A pretty spark', he was soon 'in so great splendour at court and so dandled by the King'; and Dryden, talking of the King's bastards, thought 'of all this Numerous Progeny was none, So Beautiful so Brave as *Absalon*'. He was fatally spoilt by his father: in 1663 he was created a Duke, given a large income and the Garter and married to the greatest heiress of the day, the Countess of Buccleuch (Foskett, N.P.G., No.78).

89

Samuel Cooper (1608(?)–72)

89 Frances Stuart, Duchess of Richmond (1648–1702)

Watercolour on vellum: oval, $3\frac{3}{4} \times 2\frac{7}{8}$ in., 9.5×7.3 cm.
Signed and dated: *166[ ]/SC* (initials in monogram).
Recorded at Kensington in the reign of George I. Vertue,
who noted the miniature at Kensington in 1734, gave the
date as 1663. Early in the reign of Queen Victoria it was
read as 1665. A miniature by Cooper of the Duchess in the
Uffizi, in which the face is close to No.89, is dated 1669;
but an enamel copy of No.89 by Petitot, sold at Christie's,
3 December 1963 (160), is dated 1665.

Pepys, visiting Cooper's house on 30 March 1668, saw a
recent portrait of the Duchess, just before she had had
smallpox (see No.84). On 15 July 1664 he had seen her
coming out of the Chair Room at Whitehall 'in a most
lovely form, with her hair all about her eares, having her
picture taking there'; but that is probably to be linked
with her portrait in a man's buff doublet by Huysmans. A
male riding coat had become fashionable for ladies. A year
earlier, when he had seen the King and Queen riding in
the park with the Ladies of Honour, in feathered hats,
riding habits and their hair 'dressed *a la negligence*', Pepys
regarded Mrs Stewart, 'in this dresse . . . with her sweet
eye, little Roman nose, and excellent *Taille*', as the
greatest beauty of them all. 'And if ever woman can, doth
exceed my Lady Castlemaine.' No.89 is a magnificent
example of Cooper's late style, in which he achieves a
remarkable illusion of a physical presence and a tangible
atmosphere. The handling is exceptionally refined
(D. Foskett, *Samuel Cooper* (1974), Pl.40).

Works of Art

90 Equestrian Figure of Louis XIV, French, c.1700, on an ebonized base, 1826

Equestrian bronze, with an even black patina: the base of oak veneered with ebonized wood and fitted with mounts of bronze chased and gilt, which include four female allegorical figures at the corners. Overall height, $81\frac{1}{2}$ in. (207 cm). Figure: height, $41\frac{1}{2}$ in. (105.4 cm); width, $38\frac{1}{4}$ in. (97.2 cm); depth, 21 in. (53.3 cm). Pedestal: height $40\frac{1}{4}$ in. (102.2 cm); width, 51 in. (129.5 cm); depth, $32\frac{1}{2}$ in. (82.5 cm). The figure is struck with three crowned C marks (1745–49).

The figure was bought for George IV in Paris in 1817 by François Benois, his pastry cook and agent, at a cost of £360. At the time it stood on a square ebony plinth inlaid with brass. The replacement pedestal, commissioned by Benois, was supplied by the Parisian manufacturers Thomire & Cie, and was delivered to Carlton House on 30 May 1826. It cost £281. 3s. 6d. The bas-reliefs on either side represent military triumphs of Louis XIV: The Crossing of the Rhine, 11 June 1672, and The Capture of Valenciennes, 16 March 1677, after designs by Adam-Frans Van der Meulen engraved by Charles Simonneau and Robert Bonnart.

The figure is a reduction of the bronze modelled by François Girardon and cast by J.-B. Keller which was unveiled in August 1699 in the Place Louis-le-Grand (now Place Vendôme), Paris. The figures of the horse and the rider were cast in one piece – a technical *tour de force* which was much admired at the time. Overthrown and destroyed at the Revolution, only one foot of the horse survives, preserved in the Louvre.

Whereas doubts arise as to the date of many surviving versions – copies in several sizes were made in the nineteenth century by Parisian manufacturers such as the Beurdeleys and Henri Dasson – the crowned C marks on the Royal Collection version provide a *terminus ad quem* for the date of its manufacture. As proof of the payment of a tax the crowned C had to be struck on all bronzes cast in France during the years 1745 to 1749 as well as on those in the trade at the time. Though in theory the figure could date from 1745 to 1749 it seems more likely that it was cast *c*.1700.

The provenance of the bronze is not known. Versions of the larger model, of which this is an example, which can

90

be traced back to the eighteenth century are in the Louvre and the Hermitage. The latter stands on a rectangular base similar to the one in the Royal Collection. They both have canted corners and are treated naturalistically. The version in Vaux-le-Vicomte is a later casting, though its base incorporating caryatids at the corners may date from *c*.1700; it matches the one in the engraving published in the *Galerie de Girardon* (1710). Girardon himself owned a large version. Others featured in the Paris sales of the duc de Tallard (22 March–13 May 1756 (Lot 938)), L.-J. Gaignat (14–22 Feb. 1769 (Lot 72)) and Chabot and de La Mure (17 Dec. 1787 (Lot 344)). In the lists drawn up in 1794 of confiscated works of art versions are also recorded among the possessions of the duc de Montmorency and the duc de Liancourt (AN F17*, 23 and 372).

The pedestal which Thomire & Cie provided for the Royal Collection bronze bears no relation either to the one made for the monument in the Place Louis-le-Grand or for the reduction in the *Galerie de Girardon*. The four corner figures may have been inspired by the four Virtues which flanked the pedestal of Bouchardon's equestrian figure of Louis XV inaugurated in 1763 in the Place Louis XV (now Place de la Concorde). They represented Justice, Force, Prudence and Peace.

By commissioning a pedestal in France for the equestrian bronze it was clearly intended that the pedestal should complement the statue in style and decoration. It is therefore all the more surprising to discover that the statue and its pedestal, which were despatched to Windsor on 16 September 1828, were placed in a totally alien environment, Sir Jeffry Wyatville's recently created Gothic Dining Room, where they were surrounded by tables, sideboards and a mirror frame which had been designed in an *outré* gothic style by A.W.N. Pugin (for an account of the reductions of the figure see Kunstmuseum Düsseldorf, *Europäische Barockplastik . . .* (1971), Nos.335–6; Souchal II, pp.55–6).

91 Siphon Wheel Barometer by Thomas Tompion, c.1700

Of oak and pine veneered with a burr wood (? mulberry). The mounts are of bronze chased and gilt. The shaft above the square dial plate is mounted at the top with William III's cypher (WR interlaced and crowned) and terminates in a flaming urn. Below the dial flanking the shaft are scrolled foliate mounts. The dial is pierced with two apertures for the date and the month which are

91

operated by the centre and right-hand knobs. Height, $43\frac{5}{16}$ in. (110 cm); width, $11\frac{5}{8}$ in. (29.5 cm); depth, $4\frac{1}{2}$ in. (11.4 cm). Engraved on the silvered brass dial plate: *Tho : Tompion fe/Londini* (Thomas Tompion, 1639–1713).

Made for William III probably for Hampton Court. Zacharias von Uffenbach visited Hampton Court on 24 October 1710, when he saw 'a special kind of barometer and thermometer in the form of a clock, which are made by Tomson [sic]'. Though the thermometer no longer survives, the barometer is almost certainly the one exhibited. The wheel barometer, devised by Robert Hooke and first published by him in his *Micrographia* (1665), records barometric changes by means of a hand on a dial instead of a scale. In an account entitled, *Aerostatick Instruments*, he describes how in 1678 he tried out an improved version at Thomas Tompion's, 'A person deservedly famous for his excellent skill in making Watches and Clocks, and not less Curious and deserving in the constructing and handworking of other nice mechanick Instruments' (R.W. Symonds, *Thomas Tompion . . .* (1951), pp.248–9, 295–6; N. Goodison, *English Barometers . . .* (1969), pp.232–5).

92 French Bureau with loose Drawer Section, c.1675–80

COLOUR PLATE XV opposite

Elaborately shaped bureau of oak, walnut and beech, lavishly veneered on a ground of brass with pictorial marquetry. It is composed of pewter, silver, copper, mother-of-pearl, ebony, horn, tortoise-shell, etc., in part engraved; coloured foils (red, green and blue) are used as a backing to the transparent materials. The marquetry comprises scrolls, figures, birds, animals, grotesques and architectural elements such as urns on pedestals and an obelisk. Inlaid in the centre of the top are the arms of the Gondi family; the family's badge (two crossed maces) is veneered twice on panels on top of the drawer section and four times on the lambrequins between the legs. The pegtop feet and mouldings round the top and bottom of the legs are of silvered metal. The table-top is hinged across the centre and lifts up to reveal a broad compartment concealed by three false drawer fronts. Below these, in the centre, is a hinged flap and on either side two superimposed drawers.

The eight straight fluted legs, which may be later replacements, are veneered with ebony inlaid with brass. Overall height, 38 in. (96.5 cm). Bureau: height, $30\frac{5}{16}$ in. (77 cm); width, $32\frac{1}{16}$ in. (81.5 cm); depth, $17\frac{1}{8}$ in. (43.5 cm).

The arms inlaid on the bureau have been identified with those of Paule-Françoise-Marguerite de Gondi, duchesse de Retz (born 1655). In 1675 she married François-Emmanuel de Blanchefort, duc de Lesdiguières, who died six years later. She survived him into the eighteenth century. Jean Corbinelli, however, in his genealogical history (1705) of the Gondis, indicates that after marriage she had continued to use her maiden name and the arms of her mother, Catherine de Gondi. The piece of furniture could have belonged either to the mother or the daughter.

The desk is closely related to one now in the J. Paul Getty Museum, Malibu (sold by Christie's at Wateringbury Place, 1 June 1978 (545); sold Sotheby's, Monaco, 22 June 1987 (1097). The Malibu desk lacks the loose drawer section and its proportions are slightly larger. It is supported on scrolled legs joined by stretchers, and its top is inlaid with an Italian late seventeenth-century coat of arms. The marquetry panel in the knee-hole section of both pieces is also repeated on a large Boulle-veneered dressing table in the Victoria and Albert Museum dated c.1680 (No.372-1901).

In general shape the de Retz piece and the Getty one have affinities with a table formerly in Monbijou, Berlin (W. Stengel, *Alte Wohnkultur in Berlin und in der Mark . . .*, (Berlin 1958), Fig.12a–b). This piece, which is supported on scrolled legs, retains its loose drawer section. Its polychrome marquetry is of lavish oriental inspiration which in turn recalls that of the Knole bureau (sold Christie's, London, 17 June 1987 (73)). Whereas it has been suggested that the Knole and Monbijou pieces could be of German manufacture, there can be little doubt as to the French origin of the de Retz and Getty pieces.

PLATE XV
French Bureau with loose Drawer Section (No.92)

The following pages:

PLATE XVI
Detail from an English Cabinet attributed to Gerrit Jensen (No.94)

PLATE XVII
Detail from a pair of combined Pot-Pourri Vases and Candelabra by Matthew Boulton (No.96)

93 Pair of Delft Ewers on Stands, c.1690–94

COLOUR PLATE XVIII opposite

Of tin-glazed earthenware decorated overall in two shades of blue with darker outlines. On each ewer the handle is formed by two serpents twisted like a rope; at its base is a lion head. A male mask decorates the underside of the spout of the ewer. The stand, square in section, rests on the backs of four lions holding globes, and is fitted on two sides with handles in the form of a ring held in the mouth of a lion's mask. The rim on top of the base into which the circular foot of the ewer slots is composed of four sinuous snakes. The ewer and stand are painted with rosettes, naturalistic flowers, birds and horizontal foliate bands which include palmettes. Overall height, $46\frac{1}{16}$ in. (117 cm). Ewer: height, $31\frac{1}{8}$ in. (79 cm); width, $12\frac{1}{4}$ in. (31.1 cm); depth, $11\frac{3}{4}$ in. (29.8 cm). Stand: height, $16\frac{3}{4}$ in. (42.5 cm); width, $14\frac{1}{4}$ in. (36.2 cm); depth, $14\frac{1}{4}$ in. (36.2 cm). The monogram AK is painted on the base of the ewers and on one of the stands (Adriaen Kocks, proprietor of the Greek A factory 1687–1701).

When Queen Mary II (1662–94) came to England in 1689 she was already an avid collector of porcelain – principally oriental and Delft – a taste which she had indulged in the palaces of Honselaarsdijk and Het Loo. In England her collections were kept in the main in Kensington Palace and came to fill eleven rooms. At Hampton Court she furnished a temporary building, the Water Gallery, to suit her own convenience while the major transformations were being carried out in the palace. Daniel Defoe described the Water Gallery in ecstatic terms: 'Her Majesty had here a fine Apartment, with a Sett of Lodgings for her private Retreat only, but most exquisitely furnish'd; . . . and here was also her Majesty's fine Collections of Delft Ware, which indeed was very large and fine; . . .'

Nine of the ten pieces of Delft ware at Hampton Court, which include the pair of vases exhibited, bear the mark of Adriaen Kocks. They are the sole survivors of Queen Mary's collection still in royal ownership. Some are painted with the double cypher of William and Mary.

The Queen ordered the porcelain direct from the factory (a bill, dated July 1695, one year after her death, is for a sum of £122. 14s. 9d. owing to Kocks in respect of 'China or ware sent to her late Maty'); and she set a fashion which others in the court circle followed. Delft vases and urns, many of which bear the AK monogram, are still to be found at Erddig, Dyrham Park, Chatsworth and Castle Howard. The shapes of many of these pieces, which are of distinctive design, have been attributed to Daniel Marot, the Huguenot architect and designer who was Master of Works to William III (M. Archer, 'Dutch Delft at the Court of William and Mary', *Handbook of The International Ceramics Fair and Seminar* (London, Dorchester Hotel, 1984), pp.15–20; National Gallery of Art, Washington, *Treasure Houses Of Britain . . .* (1985), Nos.102–5, entries by M. Archer).

94 English Cabinet attributed to Gerrit Jensen, c.1691–95

COLOUR PLATE XVI (detail) between pages 96 and 97

Rectangular cabinet of pine and oak, veneered with ebony and inlaid with marquetry of brass, pewter, walnut, rosewood and tortoise-shell. The marquetry includes fretwork, foliate trails, mosaic panels and urns. The cabinet is fitted with a drawer in the frieze inlaid in a roundel in the centre with a combined MR and WR cypher interlaced (brass on ebony). Below this drawer are a further six disposed in three tiers. The cabinet is supported on four tapering baluster legs, which are joined by flat angular stretchers and are each mounted with a capital of gilded wood and two mouldings of gilt bronze. Height, $33\frac{1}{2}$ in. (85.1 cm); width, $34\frac{1}{4}$ in. (87 cm); depth, $23\frac{3}{4}$ in. (60.3 cm).

As the cypher indicates, the cabinet was made for King William III and Queen Mary. It has long been attributed to Gerrit Jensen (active 1680–1715), whose name first appears in Charles II's accounts in 1680. In 1689 his appointment as Cabinet Maker in ordinary to William and Mary was renewed. In the succeeding years the furniture he supplied for the Crown consisted principally of pier glasses, as well as japanned and inlaid furniture, some of the inlays being described as composed of metal.

Jensen is the only cabinet maker working in England in the seventeenth century who is known to have specialized in furniture incorporating metal inlays in the manner of A.-C. Boulle. Professor Th.H. Lunsingh Scheurleer has identified the engraved source for the inlay on the table top. It has been faithfully copied – except for the figure scene in the central roundel – from the engraved design of a table cloth by the Huguenot architect and designer, Daniel Marot (*Nouveaux Livre d'Ornements propres pour faire en Broderie et petit point*, numbered 2). After the

PLATE XVIII
Pair of Delft Ewers on Stands (No.93)

97

94

Revocation of the Edict of Nantes in 1685, he fled to Holland and entered the service of the Prince of Orange, working for him first in Holland and then in England.

R.W. Symonds (*Connoisseur* Vol.XCV (Jan–June 1935), pp.272–3) first identified the table as the one, described in Jensen's invoice for the period Michaelmas 1694 to Lady-Day 1695, which he supplied for William III's service at Kensington Palace: 'a fine writeing desk Table Inlaid wth metall £70'. All subsequent writers have accepted Symonds's identification, but it is not self-evident. The piece of furniture is not immediately recognizable as a 'writeing desk table'. There is no outer surface on which to write; the frieze drawer is not fitted with a slide or a fall-down front; and in its construction the piece does not form a coherent whole, as has been revealed during a recent restoration in the workshops at Marlborough House. The frieze drawer projects in relation to the fore-corners. It cannot be pushed back further because of the top rail of the box-like carcase containing the drawers. The bottom of the apron section of the frieze drawer below the cypher has had to be filed off so as to release the centre top drawer of the carcase. On the underside of the carcase of the frieze section, which is built separately, are four holes, now serving no purpose, which may have been intended for the fixings for legs. The stretcher frames are pierced with single holes at their four extremities. These holes have been partly filled in in order to accommodate the dowels of the existing legs. If these later modifications are ignored, a foot extending from the centre of each unutilized hole on the underside of the frieze section would align exactly with the original centre of the corresponding hole in the stretcher. On this evidence it is possible to visualize a side table made up of the frieze section and stretcher frame joined by turned or twisted legs and resting on bun feet; the other elements would have formed another piece of furniture.

There are, however, no grounds for questioning the attribution of the cabinet or each of its components to Jensen. Even the marriage could have been carried out by Jensen. In 1691 he was transforming a reading desk into a table and later that year he charged £1. 10s. for 'altering a Desk & making a Table in it'. The William and Mary cypher would imply that it must have been made – or at least the frieze section – before the Queen's death on 28 December 1694. Unfortunately, none of the entries in Jensen's bills are sufficiently detailed and clear to allow an identification to be made with any confidence. References to 'metal Tables' and 'Table Boxes' might refer to the components of the existing cabinet, or alternatively 'a Cabinet Inlaid wth mettall and Ebony', priced at the very large sum of £150 in 1695, could apply to the piece of furniture in its present form (RA, Great Wardrobe Account Bills 1690–6; DOEFM, pp.485–7, entry by G. Jackson-Stops).

95 Pair of semi-circular Cabinets by William Gates, 1781

Of oak and pine, veneered with satinwood, tulipwood, purplewood, sycamore, amboyna and other woods, in part stained, shaded and engraved. Each cabinet is fitted with shelves closed by four doors. In the frieze are three drawers, the outer two hinged at their rear corners and the centre one covered with a slide for writing. The doors are veneered with single vases; arabesques decorate the drawer fronts and the top. Height, 35¼ in. (89.5 cm); width, 45 in. (114.3 cm); depth, 21 in. (53.3 cm). Supplied by William Gates in 1781 for the Prince of Wales's apartments in the Queen's House, St James's Park (i.e., Buckingham House).

In his bill for the quarter ending 5 April 1781 Gates describes the cabinets as, '2 very fine Sattin wood inlaid commode Tables to stand under piers with Cimi Circular fronts, 4 drawers each [sic], & 3 drawers over ditto one drawer of each with a sliding board over ditto, cover'd with green cloth to write on, . . .'. They cost £80 and the leather covers an additional £3. 1s. 6d. (PRO, LC9/328, No.25). The bespoke covers were worthy of the cabinets they were designed to protect. Cut to the shape of each cabinet, they were made of leather, and were lined and bound with gilt leather.

William Gates (active 1774–after 1800), who succeeded John Bradburn in July 1777 as Cabinet Maker to the Great Wardrobe, is first mentioned in the Royal accounts in the quarter ending Michaelmas 1777. He was actively employed on royal commissions up to c.1782. He provided a wide range of expensive furniture, principally for the Prince of Wales's apartments in Buckingham House, but also for St James's Palace, Kew Palace and Windsor Castle. Thereafter his name rarely features in the accounts though, on the evidence of a bill for the quarter ending 5 January 1790, he was acting at that time on a sub-contractual basis making furniture which John Russell had been commissioned to supply for the Prince of Wales's apartments in Buckingham House and Windsor Castle (PRO, LC9/337, No.79; DOEFM, pp.332–3, entry by T. Rosoman).

95

96

96 Pair of combined Pot-Pourri Vases and Candelabra by Matthew Boulton, c.1771

COLOUR PLATE XVII (detail) between pages 96 and 97

Each vase and cover is of blue john (Derbyshire fluor-spar); the base is of oak veneered with tortoise-shell. The mounts are of bronze chased and gilt. A pierced gilt bronze band separates the cover from the vase. Two half-figures of satyrs support the twin branch candle-arms. Height, 22½ in. (57.1 cm); width, 21¾ in. (55.2 cm); depth, 7 in. (17.8 cm).

The candelabra vases together with the pair of pot-pourri vases (No.99) and the clock (No.98) may have formed part of a *garniture de cheminée* commissioned by George III and Queen Charlotte when they met Matthew Boulton (1728–1809) for the first time in March 1770. At this meeting which lasted three hours, the Queen, whom Boulton described in a letter to his wife as 'extremely sensible, very affable, and . . . a patroness of English manufactorys, . . .' asked him to supply a set of vases to replace the china ornaments on her chimney-piece.

George III was anxious to lend his support to new projects, particularly if they favoured the development of national industries. Matthew Boulton's scheme, which he had launched two years previously, was aimed at rivalling and indeed surpassing the French in the manufacture of ornamental vases, which combine gilt bronze mounts with porcelain, marble or other materials. One aspect of his project which would have appealed to the King was the use Boulton was planning to make of an English-mined mineral for the body of many of his vases, Derbyshire fluorspar. In the spring of 1769 Boulton visited the mining areas of Derbyshire and from one supplier he bought fourteen tons of fluorspar at a cost of £81. 1s. 6d. (Goodison, pp.29–30).

George III's interest in this particular commission can plausibly be inferred from a report of Boulton's dated March 1770, in which he refers to 'a drawing [by Sir William Chambers] from a sketch of the King's for a better foot to our 4-branched vase'. It is perhaps significant that the foot, as executed, on these vases which were specially made for the King and Queen, closely resembles the feet on the clock which was also a royal commission (Goodison in FHS, vol.VIII (1972), pp.35–40; QG, 1974–5, No.26; Goodison, pp.158–61).

97 Marble-topped Table
attributed to Mayhew and Ince, c.1775

Of walnut and pine, carved and gilt and incorporating decorative elements cast in composition, also gilt. The dove-grey marble top, edged with a reeded gilt bronze moulding, is inlaid with a chequer-board pattern of 160 squares of specimen marble. The table is supported on six tapering fluted legs crowned by Ionic capitals. A tablet with a seated lion decorates the centre of the front. Height, 32¾ in. (83.2 cm); width, 57¾ in. (146.7 cm); depth, 27 in. (68.6 cm). Sold at Sotheby's, London, by the executors of Colonel Abel Henry Smith on 13 March 1931 (109), the table was bought for £200 by Queen Mary from Messrs Botibol in April 1931 for the King's private collection of furniture. It was painted white at the time, and was subsequently gilded on Queen Mary's instructions.

The table was probably made for Thomas Rumbold (1736–1791), a successful nabob in the service of the East India Company, who in 1770 returned to England after eighteen years in India. Rumbold purchased the estate of Woodhall, Hertfordshire, from the Boteler family about 1776 and immediately engaged Thomas Leverton to design a new house, which was built between 1777 and 1782. Rumbold was again in India, 1778–80. Three years after his death in 1791, the estate (including the house with its contents) was sold to another nabob, Paul Benfield, who went spectacularly bankrupt in 1801. Woodhall was then purchased by the banker Samuel Smith in whose descendants' hands it remains to the present.

It has always been assumed that, because of Rumbold's return to India in 1778, Leverton's role in the design of the furniture for Woodhall was paramount. However, the recent discovery of Rumbold's bank account (at Gosling's Bank) places the matter in a different light. Apart from two payments to John Cobb in 1772–3, the most significant disbursements are three, each of £1,000, to the leading London firm of Mayhew and Ince (10 September and 6 December 1775 and 1 June 1776). These payments pre-date the building of the new Woodhall and suggest either that Rumbold was buying furniture for the old (Boteler) house or that he was furnishing the house in Queen Anne Street, Cavendish Square, he occupied at the time of his second marriage in 1772. In either case, from the size of the payments and the roundness of the sums (certainly indicating payments on account) it seems

97

likely that Mayhew and Ince were responsible for the majority of Rumbold's new furnishings. This supposition is borne out by comparison of what has survived of the Woodhall furniture (including the present table), either in the possession of the Abel Smith family or elsewhere, with documented work by Mayhew and Ince. Even before the discovery of the payments to Mayhew and Ince, comparison had been made between this table and a pier table by Mayhew and Ince in the Metropolitan Museum of Art, New York (J. Parker, in *Decorative Art from the Samuel H. Kress Collection . . .* (1964), pp.40–2), supplied to the 6th Earl of Coventry for Croome Court, probably in 1794, at a cost of £17. 10s. Its variegated marble top had been made in 1759 by the mason and sculptor John

Wildsmith at a cost of £46. 3s. (bill dated 28 July 1759) (*Country Life* (7 Feb. 1925), pp.198–205; (26 April 1930), pp.611–13; P. Macquoid and R. Edwards, *The Dictionary of English Furniture*, vol.III (1954), p.295; Harris, Bellaigue, Millar, pp.118–19; DOEFM., pp.589–98, entry by Hugh Roberts and Charles Cator).

98

98 English Clock by Matthew Boulton, 1770–71

Of bronze chased and gilt and with panels of blue john (Derbyshire fluorspar). The square case is hung with laurel garlands suspended from rams' heads which are mounted at the corners. The case is crowned by four ewers and a two-handled vase. Height, 19$\frac{3}{16}$ in. (48.7 cm); width, 11$\frac{1}{8}$ in. (28.3 cm); depth 8$\frac{7}{16}$ in. (21.4 cm). Enamelled on the dial and engraved on the backplate: *Wright* (Thomas Wright (active *c*.1770; died 1792)).

As with the four-sided astronomical clock (No.119) Sir William Chambers designed the case in collaboration with the King. On 4 March 1770 Matthew Boulton (1728–1809) – who made the case in his Soho works – wrote to his partner informing him that Chambers was going to give him 'the King's design'.

The history of this clock has been retraced by Nicholas Goodison ('Matthew Boulton and the King's Clock Case', *Connoisseur* (June 1970), pp.77–85). The first discussions involving Matthew Boulton may have taken place on 5 March 1770. On that day he had breakfast with Chambers when, as we already know, he was expecting to receive 'the King's design'. Later that same day he dined with Thomas Wright. The problems of manufacture could not, however, all be resolved over a meal. Difficulties arose. Delays were experienced. The movement would not fit the case, so adjustments had to be made to the latter. Wright proved dilatory, to the intense vexation of Boulton, who on 22 March 1771 was describing Wright's conduct as shabby. Delivery was finally made in April 1771.

Boulton was anxious to extract every advantage from the successful manufacture of this clock for the King of England. Not content with proudly proclaiming his success to all and sundry, he had cast, unbeknown to the King, a duplicate in his workshop with a view to selling it at auction; but he was prevailed upon to abandon the project '. . . your having a clock to sell at an auction of the same pattern with his Majesty's will be an affront to his Majesty as he should have given you his permission before you had copy'd his drawing . . .' (see Goodison, pp.112–18).

99 Pair of Pot-Pourri Vases
by Matthew Boulton, c.1771

Each vase and cover is of blue john (Derbyshire fluorspar) and the mounts are of bronze chased and gilt. The band between the vase and cover is pierced. The vase is raised on two plinths, the upper one faced with lacquered glass resting on the backs of four sphinxes, the lower one veneered with tortoise-shell. Height, 12$\frac{1}{2}$ in. (31.7 cm); width, 5$\frac{3}{4}$ in. (14.6 cm); depth, 5$\frac{3}{4}$ in. (14.6 cm).

Made for George III and Queen Charlotte by Matthew Boulton (1728–1809), they may have formed part of a *garniture* supplied to the Queen in 1771. For further details see No.96 and Goodison, pp.163–5.

99

100 Pair of Console Tables
attributed to Adam Weisweiler, c.1786

Of oak and pine veneered with tulipwood, mahogany, purplewood and boxwood and fitted with mounts of bronze chased and gilt. The top is of white Carrara marble. The frieze contains three drawers, the centre one mounted with a plaque chased with putti engaged in mathematical and astronomical studies. The table is supported on fluted columns at the front and on fluted pilasters at the back flanking a glass panel. They rest on a shelf veneered with geometric marquetry above four tapering peg-top feet of solid tulipwood. Height, 35 in. (88.9 cm); width, $51\frac{3}{4}$ in. (131.5 cm); depth, $19\frac{1}{4}$ in. (48.9 cm).

The tables form part of a set of four. Though unstamped they can be attributed on stylistic grounds to Adam Weisweiler (maître-ébéniste, 1778–1820). The lush acanthus scrolls decorating the drawer fronts are, however, later embellishments, added for George IV by Benjamin Vulliamy at a cost of twenty-one guineas per table. In his bill, dated 18 June 1811, Vulliamy specifies that the mounts had been copied 'from a design & patterns made on purpose'. A later alteration was the replacement of the original spirally fluted feet – which can be seen in a drawing, forming part of George IV's Pictorial Inventory, c.1827–8, reproducing one of the tables – by the existing plain peg-top feet of solid tulipwood.

The date of purchase of these tables by George IV is not known, but it may well be that they were acquired in the late 1780s through the intermediary of Dominique Daguerre, the fashionable Parisian marchand-mercier, when he was employed by the Prince to help furnish Carlton House (for an account of Weisweiler's close association with Daguerre see Patricia Lemonnier, Weisweiler (Paris, 1983)). Although the description is very slight, it may be that they are the tables listed in the Gallery of Carlton House in 1792. In the late 1820s the four tables stood in the Dining-Room, Basement Floor at Carlton House (G. de Bellaigue in FHS, vol.XXI (1985), pp.203–4).

100

101

102

**101 Dying Gladiator, French,
seventeenth or early eighteenth century**

Bronze male figure, with a dark brown patina. The warrior, mortally wounded, has fallen to the ground and half supports himself on his right arm. Beneath him is his oval shield and a curved horn and beside him is another horn and a sword. Height, $10\frac{1}{2}$ in. (26.7 cm); width, $20\frac{1}{4}$ in. (51.4 cm); depth, $9\frac{1}{16}$ in. (23 cm).

The bronze is a reduction of the antique marble statue, probably dating from the third century B.C., first recorded in an inventory of the Ludovisi Collection in Rome in 1623 and now in the Musei Capitolini, Rome. It has remained one of the most admired antique figures. Numerous reductions in bronze were cast in the seventeenth and eighteenth centuries in both Italy and France (Haskell and Penny, No.44).

Although not recorded among George IV's purchases, it may nevertheless have been one of his acquisitions. It was in store in Carlton House in 1824.

**102 Pair of Japanese Pot-Pourri Bowls and Covers
with French Mounts, late eighteenth century**

The outside of each bowl is of black lacquer divided into four compartments by gold lines with trees in gold in each compartment. A Greek Key band in gold on black runs

round the top of the bowl on the outside and inside. The rest of the inside of the bowl and the underside of the cover are in red lacquer decorated with scrolling branches in gold. The mounts include two heads and a pierced foliate band of interlocking lozenges and circles. Height, $9\frac{7}{8}$ in. (25.1 cm); width, $9\frac{7}{16}$ in. (24 cm); diameter, $8\frac{1}{8}$ in. (20.7 cm).

This pair of pot-pourris cannot be readily identified in George IV's papers, but they were almost certainly acquired by him, possibly through Dominique Daguerre after he had been taken on in 1787 to help furnish Carlton House. Later George IV was to buy a number of mounted lacquer boxes, coffers and vases, some from the Parisian dealers, Rocheux and Lafontaine, some at auction sales in London, and some through purchases made by François Benois, on his periodic shopping trips to Paris.

103 Jewel Cabinet by Jean-Henri Riesener, c.1785
COLOUR PLATE XIX (detail) facing page 112

Of oak veneered with mahogany and fitted with mounts of bronze chased gilt. The two tazzas flanking the cresting and the two urns between the legs are in part of blued metal. The cabinet is built in three stages: the topmost one incorporates in the centre a group of three putti supporting the arms conjoined of the comte and comtesse de Provence below a coronet; the middle stage contains three drawers in the frieze, with below two doors which open to reveal a nest of three compartments and ten drawers; the bottom stage contains three drawers, and is supported on eight legs in two groups of four formed by quivers of arrows and joined above the feet by a platform supporting an urn. Height, $96\frac{7}{8}$ in. (246 cm); width, $57\frac{7}{8}$ in. (147 cm); depth, $21\frac{1}{2}$ in. (54.6 cm). Stamped: *J-H.RIESENER* (Jean-Henri Riesener, *maître-ébéniste*, 1768–1806). Bought by George IV for 400 guineas at the George Watson Taylor sale (Christie's, 28 May 1825 (76)).

The jewel cabinet was made for the comtesse de Provence (*née* Marie-Josèphe-Louise de Savoie) who married in 1771 the comte de Provence, Louis XVI's younger brother who was to ascend the throne in 1815 as Louis XVIII.

The cabinet stood in her apartments in the Palace of the Petit-Luxembourg in Paris. It was confiscated by the Revolutionary government in 1793 by virtue of a decree authorizing the seizure of the possessions of those who had been condemned to death or who had fled the country. At that time it was excluded from the possessions made available to the comte de Provence's creditors, being judged of such high quality that it had to be retained for display in the Republic's museums. Three years later, however, when the country was in desperate financial straits the decision was reversed and it was advertised for sale in the periodical, *Affiches, annonces et avis divers*, on 27 *thermidor an* IV (14 August 1796) and on two subsequent occasions that year (information kindly supplied by Christian Baulez). By the end of 1796 it had been sold. It passed through a number of hands before it was offered in 1809 by the 'femme Aulmont' to Napoleon for 30,000 francs, half the sum she claimed she had had to pay for its purchase. The offer was not taken up. Two years later comte P-A-N-B. Daru, Master of the Emperor's Household, sought permission to buy the jewel cabinet for the Palace of Saint-Cloud. Napoleon's reply, as noted by Daru in the margin of the letter, was laconic and unequivocal: 'S.M. veut faire du neuf et non acheter du vieux' (Fernand Calmettes, in *La Revue de l'Art Ancien et Moderne* (July–Dec. 1913), pp.201–13; F.J.B. Watson, in *Connoisseur Coronation Book* (1953), pp.63–5; QG, 1966, No.45).

104

104 Nymph with a Shell, French, seventeenth or early eighteenth century

Bronze female figure, with a dark brown patina. She is partly draped and is represented by the shore, half reclining and scooping water with a shell held in her right hand. Shells and algae lie scattered by the water's edge forming the oval base. Height, 11⅛ in. (28.3 cm); width, 19¼ in. (49 cm); depth, 8¹⁵⁄₁₆ in. (22.7 cm).

A reduction of the marble statue by Antoine Coysevox, executed 1683–5, originally placed by the Bassin de Latone in the gardens of Versailles (Souchal I, p.190), is now in the Louvre. It is an enlarged and slightly modified copy of an antique sculpture dating from the second century B.C. which is recorded in 1638 in the Villa Borghese, Rome. The antique was particularly admired in the seventeenth and eighteenth centuries, being reproduced in small bronzes and in biscuit Sèvres porcelain (Haskell and Penny, No.67).

Although this bronze cannot be identified in the Carlton House Receipts Ledger (commencing 31 December 1806), it could well have been acquired by George IV. It was in store in Carlton House in 1824.

105 Bust of the Emperor Charles V, attributed to Leone Leoni, mid-sixteenth century

Bronze bust, chased and engraved, with a brown patina. The Emperor wears the collar and badge of the Order of the Golden Fleece over a suit of armour in the North Italian style, which is engraved with foliate decoration. The suit is fitted with a lance rest. Height, 37½ in. (95.2 cm); width, 24½ in. (62.2 cm). Inscribed in relief in a cartouche on the socle: *IMP CAES/V/CAR AVG*. Bought by George IV for eighty-five guineas at the George Watson Taylor sale (Christie's, 28 May 1825 (65) together with two other bronzes attributed to Leone Leoni of Philip II and the Duke of Alba (67 and 69)).

Leoni, sculptor and medallist, entered the service of the Emperor Charles V (1500–58) around 1547 and executed a number of bronzes, medals and marble sculpture for the Emperor and for his son, Philip II. Several busts closely related to the Royal Collection version are known, which now form part of the collections of the Prado, Madrid, of the Kunsthistorisches Museum, Vienna and of the Château de Gaasbeek in Belgium. Some incorporate a socle composed of an eagle flanked by male and female

105

106

figures. Ulrich Middeldorf has convincingly argued that the three busts which were acquired by George IV at the Watson Taylor sale can be identified with the three commissioned by Charles V's general, Fernando Alvares de Toledo, Duke of Alba (1508–82). The commission was recorded by Vasari and the busts were seen by Cean Bermudez in 1800 in the palace of the Duke at Alba de Tormes. The Palace was destroyed at the Battle of Salamanca in 1812 (see E. Plon, *Leone Leoni . . . et Pompeo Leoni . . .* (Paris, 1887), pp.297–8; U. Middeldorf 'On some portrait busts attributed to Leone Leoni', *Burl. Mag.*, vol.CXVII (Feb. 1975), pp.88–91).

106 Two Indian Ivory Chairs, c.1770

Of sandalwood veneered with engraved ivory and fitted with cane seats. The engraved decoration, filled with black mastic, includes conventional acanthus foliage, leaf trails, flower sprigs, and oriental monster heads, their fangs highlighted in red. Height, $39\frac{1}{8}$ in. (99.4 cm); width, $24\frac{1}{2}$ in. (62.2 cm); depth, $22\frac{1}{8}$ in. (56.2 cm).

Queen Charlotte was an enthusiastic collector of oriental jewellery, porcelain, textiles and furniture. As early as 1762 she had been presented with two pagodas and a large quantity of Indian furniture. In 1785 Warren Hastings's wife gave her an ivory state bed, and fourteen years later Lord Wellesley presented her with a table and two chairs which had belonged to Tipu Sultan. After her death the gifts from Mrs Hastings and Lord Wellesley were

107

included with other works of art among the items destined for her four unmarried daughters, the princesses Charlotte, Augusta, Elizabeth and Sophia (RA, 36821–5). The bulk of her collection was, however, auctioned at Christie's in May–August 1819. Among the furniture were twenty lots comprising forty-three pieces of Indian ivory-veneered furniture, of which these are part. George IV bought fourteen chairs, two corner armchairs and two sofas (probably Lots 107 and 108 of 7 May 1819, and Lots 104 and 105 of 8 May). They were sent to Brighton Pavilion and were placed in the Long Gallery, where they can be recognized in Augustus Pugin's engraving of this room, published on 1 December 1824. Later, on 20 May 1829, George IV bought back at Lord Gwydir's sale at Christie's a pair of solid ivory arm-chairs, different in decoration but which had also belonged to Queen Charlotte (Lot 70; bought by E.H. Baldock for George IV; probably Lot 90 of the Queen Charlotte sale on 24 May 1819).

The early history of the ivory furniture acquired by

George IV in 1819 has been published by Clifford Smith (pp.218–9). They were made in Madras in about 1770, in an Indian variation of the Chippendale style, for Alexander Wynch, Governor of Fort St George. In October 1781, following his death, they were included in the sale held by Christie's of the contents of his country seat, West-thorpe House near Marlow, and were bought by George III for Queen Charlotte (QG, 1974–5, No.7).

107 Jewel Cabinet by William Vile, 1762

Of oak and mahogany veneered with tulipwood, mahogany, amboyna, rosewood, holly, olive, padouk, and engraved ivory. The hinged top, inlaid with the arms of King George III and Queen Charlotte, gives access to a compartment lined with black velvet for jewellery. The top is secured by a concealed catch which can only be operated when the two doors are opened. They reveal a nest of eight drawers. Below the doors is a further drawer secured by a lock. The cabinet is elaborately veneered on its outer surface as well as on the inside of the doors with trophies, wreaths, flowers and foliate assymetrical cartouches. Height, $42\frac{1}{2}$ in. (108 cm); width, 32 in. (81.3 cm); depth, 22 in. (55.9 cm). The door lock is stamped: *E. GASCOIGNE* (active *c.*1760–90).

On 26 July 1761 the Countess of Northumberland saw at Lady Bute's Queen Charlotte's jewels ('except those for the Head') which the King had purchased from his uncle, the Duke of Cumberland, and which had formerly belonged to Queen Caroline. The Countess was amazed at the prodigious size and most beautiful colour of the pearls. She described the stomacher, valued at £60,000, as 'the finest piece of Magnificence & Workmanship I ever saw'. Allan Ramsay's state portrait of the Queen shows her wearing some of this splendid array of jewels.

It was for this *parure* that William Vile (*c.*1700/05–1767), who received the Royal Warrant in January 1761, was commissioned to supply a jewel cabinet of appropriate

PLATE XIX
Detail from a Jewel Cabinet by Jean-Henri Riesener (No.103)

The following pages:

PLATE XX
One of a pair of matching Clocks of Chelsea Porcelain (No.113)

PLATE XXI
Pair of Crab Salts by Nicholas Sprimont (No.116)

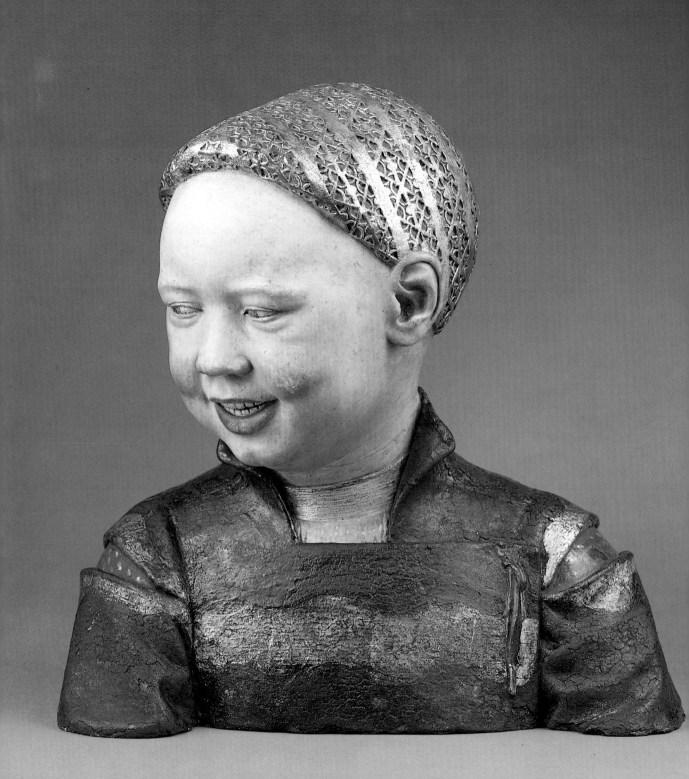

108

splendour to stand in the Queen's apartments, St James's Palace. It cost £138.10s. and is described in Vile's account for the last quarter of 1762 as 'a very handsome Jewel Cabinet made of many different kinds of fine Woods on a Mohogany frame very richly Carved . . . inlaid with Ivory in Compartments and . . . lined with fine Black Velvet . . .'. The jewels for which it was intended, repeatedly transformed by later sovereigns, eventually passed in 1858 to the King of Hanover (Shirley Bury, 'Queen Victoria and the Hanoverian Claim to the Crown Jewels', *Handbook of the International Silver & Jewellery Fair & Seminar* (London, Dorchester Hotel, 1988), pp.9–16)). On Queen Charlotte's death in 1818 the cabinet became the property of her fourth daughter, Mary, Duchess of Gloucester, from whom it passed by descent to George, Marquess of Cambridge, who sold it to Queen Mary. In a note dated

September 1951 the Queen records that she had bought the cabinet for £5,000 and presented it to King George VI for his personal collection for display in the Corridor at Windsor Castle (QG, 1974–7, No.36; V&A, *Rococo*, No.L60; DOEFM, pp.923–8, entry by Geoffrey Beard).

108 Roll-top Desk attributed to Jean-Henri Riesener, c.1775–80

Of oak veneered with purplewood, mahogany (*boissatiné*), casuarina wood, holly, box, sycamore and other woods in part stained and engraved. The mounts are of bronze chased and gilt. The desk, which is fitted with two pairs of candelabra, contains, in the frieze, a pull-out reading stand flanked by two drawers. Behind the roll-top is a nest in three tiers comprising three trays flanked on each side by three drawers. Concealed beneath the bottom tray is a hinged flap which gives access to a secret compartment. The lower half, supported on cabriole legs ending in lion's paw feet, contains a shallow centre drawer with, on either side, two drawers; they can only be opened

when the roll-top is pushed fully back. The desk is
veneered with geometric marquetry in simulated relief
enclosing water-lilies on a harewood ground and with
panels of flowers and fruit. Inlaid in a trapeze-shaped
reserve on the roll-top is a trophy emblematic of Poetry
and Literature. Height, $50\frac{3}{4}$ in. (129 cm); width, $54\frac{5}{16}$ in.
(138 cm); depth, $31\frac{7}{8}$ in. (81 cm). Bought by George IV
for 102 guineas at the George Watson Taylor sale
(Christie's, 28 May 1825 (49)). It is described in the sale
catalogue as having belonged to Louis XVI – a claim
which remains unsubstantiated.

Although unstamped the desk can be attributed to Jean-
Henri Riesener (*maître-ébéniste*, 1768–1806). It bears all
the hallmarks of his style and workshop practice: the
mechanical locking device designed to ensure that the
principal drawers are automatically locked when the
roll-top is closed. Many of the mounts and marquetry
compositions are repeated on other pieces made by
Riesener: the marquetry panel emblematic of Poetry and
Literature veneered on the roll-top is repeated on the top
of a very similar desk delivered on 30 December 1773 for
the comtesse de Provence's apartments in Versailles, and
on the top of a table made in 1777 for Louis XVI's study
in the Petit Trianon. Even in the case of the bouquets of
flowers the same compositions can also be found on other
pieces (*The James A. de Rothschild Collection at
Waddesdon Manor*, G. de Bellaigue, *Furniture Clocks and
Gilt Bronzes* (Fribourg, 1974), vol.I, pp.297–307, vol.II,
pp.504–9).

George Watson Taylor (?1770–1841), the son of a West
India proprietor, had inherited through his wife a vast
fortune which he spent on pictures and works of art and
on the purchase and embellishment of his town house in
Cavendish Square and his country seat, Erlestoke Park,
near Devizes, Wiltshire. A victim of his own extravagance
and of the fall in value of West India property, he was
obliged to dispose of his collections in sales held by
Christie's in 1823 and 1825 and by George Robins in
1832. George IV seized this opportunity of enriching his
collection and on 28 May 1825 bid successfully for
twenty-nine lots of furniture and bronzes. In making
these purchases George IV did not have Carlton House in
mind but Windsor Castle. 'It (the furniture) is quite
appropriate for Windsor Castle', George IV wrote to
the Duke of Wellington in a letter dated 16 February
1828 (*Correspondence of George Prince of Wales*, ed.
A. Aspinall, vol.VIII (1971), p.475) (Harris, Bellaigue,
Millar, pp.204–5).

109

114

109 Psyche and Mercury attributed to Philippe Bertrand, early eighteenth century

Bronze group, with a dark brown patina. Mercury, balancing on the edge of a cloud, holds aloft his caduceus in his left hand. With his right he lightly touches Psyche who prepares to accompany him. She holds in her raised left hand a small covered phial. Lying prostrate at the feet of Mercury is an emaciated old woman clutching a (?) flaming torch. Overall height, 31 in. (78.7 cm); height without caduceus, $24\frac{1}{4}$ in. (61.6 cm); width, $16\frac{1}{4}$ in. (41.3 cm); depth, $11\frac{1}{4}$ in. (28.6 cm). Bought by George IV from the London silversmiths, Rundell, Bridge and Rundell, for £145 (RA 26059, bill dated 16 August 1824).

The group has been attributed to the Parisian sculptor Philippe Bertrand (1663–1724), who exhibited a bronze of this subject in the *Salon* of 1704. Another version, but without the caduceus, is in The Hermitage, Leningrad (Souchal I, pp.49–51).

The subject of this group has not been firmly established. As has been pointed out by Jennifer Montagu, if Mercury is carrying off Psyche to be married to Cupid, she should not be represented holding the pot containing a part of Proserpina's beauty, which she had already handed to Venus. Nor is the emaciated old woman readily identifiable; if it is a torch which she is holding she could personify Anger (the anger of Venus).

110 Hercules, Antaeus and Gaea, French, (?) early eighteenth century

Bronze group, with a mottled dark brown patina. Hercules, having lifted the giant Antaeus from the ground, crushes him in the air. Half emerging out of the ground is the distraught figure of Antaeus's mother, Gaea, the goddess who personified the earth. Height, $25\frac{1}{2}$ in. (64.8 cm); width, $13\frac{1}{2}$ in. (34.3 cm); depth, 10 in. (25.4 cm). Bought by George IV from the London silversmiths, Rundell, Bridge and Rundell for £63 (RA 26059, bill dated 16 August 1824).

Antaeus was invincible so long as he remained in contact with the earth. By lifting him off the ground Hercules was able to neutralize his strength. The inclusion in this group of the three-quarter figure of Gaea is unusual, as is the treatment of the ground inhabited by animals and reptiles, some erupting out of the earth.

110

111 Tureen and cover

111 Pieces from a Chelsea Porcelain Service, 1763

Of soft-paste bone-ash porcelain, decorated in under-glaze mazarine blue, enamel colours and gilding. Of elaborate rococo shape the components are painted with garlands of flowers, butterflies and birds, some in landscape settings. Oil and vinegar stand with cut glass bottles: height, $11\frac{13}{16}$ in. (30 cm); width, $10\frac{7}{16}$ in. (26.5 cm). Cruet: height, $12\frac{7}{16}$ in. (31.7 cm); width, $8\frac{11}{16}$ in. (22 cm). Tureen and cover: height, $9\frac{5}{8}$ in. (24.5 cm); width, $12\frac{13}{16}$ in. (32.5 cm); depth, $7\frac{5}{16}$ in. (18.5 cm). Sauce boat: height, $6\frac{7}{8}$ in. (17.5 cm); length, $8\frac{9}{16}$ in. (21.8 cm); width, $4\frac{9}{16}$ in. (11.6 cm). Salt cellar: height, $3\frac{1}{4}$ in. (8.3 cm); width, $4\frac{3}{4}$ in. (12 cm); depth, $3\frac{3}{8}$ in. (8.5 cm). Round plate: diameter, $9\frac{1}{4}$ in. (23.5 cm). Oval plate: width, $10\frac{13}{16}$ in. (27.5 cm); depth, $8\frac{11}{16}$ in. (22.1 cm). Gold anchor marks (period $c.1758–c.1769$).

Commissioned by King George III and Queen Charlotte, the service was presented in 1763 to the Queen's brother, Duke Adolphus Frederick IV of Mecklenburg-Strelitz. In a much quoted letter to Sir Horace Mann, 4 March 1763, Horace Walpole described it as a 'magnificent service of Chelsea china', but then goes on to criticize it: 'I cannot boast of our taste; the forms are neither new, beautiful, nor various. Yet Sprimont, the manufacturer, is a Frenchman: it seems their taste will not bear transplanting . . .' Nicholas Sprimont (1713–71) was in fact of Flemish extraction, the son of a silversmith in Liège, and in 1742 came to London, where he first practised as a silversmith (see Nos.115–19). He acquired the Chelsea porcelain factory in about 1747.

The service remained in the Mecklenburg-Strelitz family till 1919. Some additions (or replacements) had been made in the nineteenth century in Berlin in hard-paste porcelain. The service was bought by Sir Joseph (later Lord) Duveen and then passed into the possession, $c.1944$, of James Oakes, who presented it to Her Majesty Queen Elizabeth, The Queen Mother, in 1947.

The service, rightly regarded as one of the finest examples of table ware in the English rococo style, cost £1,150 (Walpole's figure was £1,200). In March 1764 the factory advertised in its sale a service of matching design which shortly thereafter was exhibited by the dealer Williams. John Mallet has suggested that pieces belonging to the second service can be distinguished from the original as the decoration of the later service incorporates mazarine blue panels indented as opposed to rounded at the rim (QG, 1974–5, No.50; V&A, *Rococo*, No.039, entry by J.V.G. Mallet).

112 Pair of Chelsea Pot-Pourri Vases, c.1765–70

Of soft-paste bone-ash porcelain decorated in underglaze mazarine blue, enamel colours and gilding. Each pear-shaped vase rests on four scrolled feet and is fitted with pierced foliate handles. Fan-shaped openings are pierced in the neck and attached cover. The body of the vase is painted with genre scenes in the manner of Nicolas Lancret. Height, $13\frac{1}{2}$ in. (34.3 cm); width, $5\frac{7}{8}$ in. (14.8 cm); depth, $5\frac{5}{16}$ in. (13.5 cm). On one, a gold anchor mark (period $c.1758–c.1769$).

According to Clifford Smith (p.205) these vases formed part of Queen Charlotte's collections. Though their exuberant rococo shape and decoration would have accorded with the Queen's taste – they are very much in the same spirit as the Queen's Chelsea clocks (No.113) and the service she gave to her brother (No.111) – it has not been possible to trace them in the Christie's catalogues of her sales held in 1819. A single vase, which may well have been of the same shape as the pair in the Royal Collection, was Lot 32 of Queen Charlotte's sale on 11 May 1819. It was however painted with a scene of men smoking.

112

113 Two matching Clocks of Chelsea Porcelain, c.1760–65

COLOUR PLATE XX between pages 112 and 113

Of soft-paste bone-ash porcelain decorated with a deep crimson ground, enamel colours and gilding. Springing from a scrolled oval base is an asymmetrical arch which supports the hood, which is scrolled and winged on one side. Cupid gazes down on a sleeping shepherdess, who is about to be awakened by her lover. Height, 17 in. (43.2 cm); width, 12½ in. (31.7 cm); depth, 9 in. (22.8 cm). On one gold anchor mark (period c.1758–c.1769). Painted in black enamel on each dial: *STRIGEL/LONDON* and engraved on the backplate of one movement (the other missing): *Geo. Phi. Strigel/London* (G.P. Strigel, 1718–98). The clocks belonged to Queen Charlotte, at whose death they were acquired by George IV for 70 guineas (Christie's, 11 May 1819 (47)).

Clock cases of porcelain are first recorded in Europe in the 1720s. The earliest known example, which is dated 1725, was made in the Du Paquier factory in Vienna. At Chelsea clock cases were being produced during the later 1750s. John Mallet, who associates No.112 with the style of Joseph Willems, has proposed a *terminus ad quem* of 1766, the year that Willems left for Tournai ('Chelsea Porcelain – Botany and Time', *Handbook of The Burlington House Antiques Fair* (1980), pp.12–13). Another version which has affinities with Queen Charlotte's pair was sold at Sotheby's, London, 17 July 1973 (109). It too bears the gold anchor mark (V&A, *Rococo*, No.042, entry by J.V.G. Mallet).

114 Centrepiece by Paul Crespin, 1741/2

Of silver-gilt elaborately chased with shells, seaweed, pearls, masks, coral, strapwork and scrolls. The oval tureen, garlanded on the body and cover with crustaceans and marine plants, is flanked by two figures, a merman at one end and a mermaid at the other. They are each seated on a shell and hold aloft a marine garland. The knob of the cover is formed by a seated figure of Poseidon. The tureen and the flanking figures are supported on double scrolled members which spring from the back of four dolphins and are accompanied by four twisted candle arms; these are fitted with loose coral-encrusted covers. The whole rests on an asymmetrical base chased on its jagged edge with coral, shells, and plants and incorporating rock-like troughs in the centre of the front and back. The Royal Arms, as used between 1816 and 1837, have been added in the centre of the base. Height, 19½ in. (49.5 cm); width, 26 in. (66 cm); depth, 18⅝ in. (47.3 cm): Hallmarked 1741/2, it bears the maker's mark of Paul Crespin (1713–70). The mark of John Bridge has been struck on four straps on the underside of the base. The straps serve as fixings for a stand supported by four hippocampi (not exhibited), which was added c.1826.

The centrepiece and the salts displayed in this showcase were almost certainly commissioned by Frederick, Prince of Wales (1707–51). They and the other silver-gilt pieces exhibited are identified for the first time, as part of his service, in an inventory made for William IV in 1832.

Frederick, Prince of Wales, formed an important collection of silver principally through his patronage of the goldsmith, George Wickes, appointed Goldsmith to the Prince in 1735. His ledgers survive from that date. Commissions placed with one craftsman were frequently sub-contracted in part or in whole to others. Elaine Barr, in line with Arthur Grimwade, suggests that it is not inconceivable that an entry in Wickes's ledger dated 24 June 1742 for a costly 'Surtout Compleat' might refer to the centrepiece. Elaine Barr has suggested that the surtout could have been sent to Nicholas Sprimont in Liège for finishing before he finally took up residence in London later in 1742; but points out that the evidence is still too fragmentary to allow any conclusions to be drawn (A. Grimwade, *Rococo Silver . . .* (1974), pp.30–1; V&A, *Rococo*, G17, pp.113–4, entry by E. Barr).

114

115

115

115 Four Sauceboats by Nicholas Sprimont, 1743/4

Of silver-gilt, the bowl of each, half shell, half boat, is supported on the back of a dolphin resting on an asymmetrical coral and shell-encrusted base. A seated figure – male on two and female on the other two – serves as the handle. Height, $8\frac{15}{16}$ in. (22.7 cm) and $9\frac{1}{8}$ in. (23.2 cm); width, $8\frac{1}{16}$ in. (20.6 cm); depth, $5\frac{1}{16}$ in. (13 cm). Hallmarked 1743/4, they each bear the maker's mark of Nicholas Sprimont who was active as a silversmith from 1742(?) to 1747. Part of Frederick, Prince of Wales's, service (see No.114). The dolphins are treated very much in the same spirit as those on the centrepiece bearing Paul Crespin's mark (V&A, *Rococo*, G17, p.114, entry by E. Barr). Copies were made in 1780 by Robert Hennell and in 1819–20 by Robert Garrard.

116 Pair of Crab Salts by Nicholas Sprimont, 1742/3

COLOUR PLATE XXI between pages 112 and 113

Of silver-gilt. Each is in the form of an irregular pierced platform, chased with coral, shells and algae, which supports a prominent conch shell and a crab. The shell serves as the salt cellar. The platform is raised on three shell-encrusted coral lumps. Height, $3\frac{1}{2}$ in. (8.9 cm); width, 7 in., (17.8 cm); depth, $4\frac{5}{8}$ in. (11.7 cm). Hallmarked 1742/3, they each bear the maker's mark of Nicholas Sprimont. Part of Frederick, Prince of Wales's, service, they accompany the centrepiece and the pair of crayfish salts (Nos.114 and 117).

The four silver-gilt spoons (length, $4\frac{5}{8}$ in. (11 cm)) are unmarked. They have fluted bowls in the form of clams and stems shaped like forked branches. They resemble a sketch of one of two spoons flanking a rococo salt cellar by the carver and gilder, Matthias Lock. The drawing dates from about 1740 (A. Grimwade, *Rococo Silver . . .* (1974), pp.45, Pl.37c).

117 Two Crayfish Salts by Nicholas Sprimont, 1742/3

Of silver-gilt, each is in the form of a fluted shell with a serrated lip which rests on a rock chased with small shells and coral. A crayfish straddles the rock. Height, $3\frac{7}{16}$ in. (8.7 cm); width, $5\frac{1}{2}$ in. (14 cm); depth, $5\frac{9}{16}$ in. (14.1 cm). Hallmarked 1742/3, they each bear the maker's mark of Nicholas Sprimont.

Part of Frederick, Prince of Wales's, service (see No. 114). So realistic is the modelling of the crayfish and the crabs on the companion salts (No. 116) that they may have been cast from the life. The model was repeated in porcelain at the Chelsea factory which Sprimont acquired *c.*1747. Some versions are merely glazed, others are coloured. They range in date from the Triangle Period (*c.*1745–49) to the Red Anchor Period (*c.*1752–58) (V&A, *Rococo*, G17, p.114, entry by E. Barr; O7, p.245, entry by J.V.G. Mallet).

117

118 Mermen Salt attributed to Nicholas Sprimont, c.1742–5

Of silver-gilt, in the form of a flat shell with a trail of shells and algae extending across the top and into the bowl. It is supported at three points, on two young tritons and on a shell-encrusted lump of coral. Height, $2\frac{5}{8}$ in. (6.7 cm); width, $8\frac{1}{4}$ in. (21 cm); depth, $5\frac{15}{16}$ in. (15 cm). Unmarked.

One of a pair of salts which form part of Frederick, Prince of Wales's, service (see No. 114) and may have been made by Nicholas Sprimont (V&A, *Rococo*, cited by E. Barr, p.114).

118

119 Dragon Salt attributed to Nicholas Sprimont, c.1742–5

Of silver gilt. A dragon on a flat, rocky base supports on its wings and tail the salt cellar, in the form of a large open shell. A lizard crawls along the top of the shell which is encrusted with a trail of algae and crustaceans. Height, $4\frac{1}{2}$ in. (11.5 cm); width, $7\frac{9}{16}$ in. (19.2 cm); depth, $7\frac{1}{4}$ in. (18.5 cm). Unmarked.

One of a pair of salts which forms part of Frederick, Prince of Wales's, service (see No. 114) and may have been made by Nicholas Sprimont (V&A, *Rococo*, cited by E. Barr, p.114).

119

120 Four-sided astronomical Clock
by Christopher Pinchbeck and others, 1768
COLOUR PLATE XXIV after page 132

Of oak veneered with tortoise-shell on a red foil and fitted with elaborately chased gilt bronze and silver mounts. The domed case is in the form of a temple, the entablature supported at each corner on a pilaster and two columns which are partly fluted and which terminate in Corinthian capitals. The four dials show, respectively, on the front: the time of day on a twenty-four hour dial with hands for mean and solar time; it also shows the time at various places of different longitude throughout the world; on the back: the tides at forty-three points (mostly in the British Isles) and the phases of the moon; on the left: the days of the week and of the month, the position of the sun and by means of a planisphere the position of the stars; on the right: an orrery showing the motions of six planets, Mercury, Venus, Earth, Mars, Jupiter and Saturn, as well as a metallic thermometer graduated from 25 to 85. Height, $30\frac{5}{8}$ in. (77.8 cm); diameter of base, $20\frac{1}{4}$ in. (51.4 cm). Enamelled in black on the orrery dial: *C.PINCHBECK / SUSCEPIT / I. MERIGEOT. I.MONK PERFECERUNT* (Christopher Pinchbeck (1710–83) assisted by John Merigeot (apprenticed to the clockmaker, George Somersall in 1742) and John Monk (apprenticed in 1762)).

On 29 January 1768 Lady Mary Coke and Lady Strafford visited Pinchbeck 'to see a very fine Clock that was just finisht for his Majesty. 'Twas well worth seeing. The Clock is itself very curious, but too complicated a piece of workmanship to be easily described. The case is magnificent, the execution extremely fine, & the design partly His Majesty's, & partly Mr Chambers his Architect.' Chambers's involvement is confirmed by a drawing of the case in the Sir John Soane Museum, which was identified by John Harris and attributed by him to Chambers. It is not however clear how George III contributed to the design of the case. Perhaps he was responsible for the first outline sketch, or he may have modified Chambers's design. In this context it may be significant that the Soane Museum sketch departs from the clock as executed in a number of respects. The actual maker of the case, however, is unknown. The mounts are jewel-like in their chasing. To take one example, each leaf of the capitals is cast separately and attached by concealed screws. The setting-out on a drawing board of the case before it was built must have been carried out with as much precision as if it were a building which was being designed rather than a piece of furniture. The case is made up of a complex web of interlocking components which fit together like a Chinese puzzle.

The clock was placed in the Passage Room leading from the Hall to the Garden at Buckingham House. A pedestal of gilded wood, probably designed by Chambers, was made to support it. It is no longer in the Collection. Of unusual design, it was in the form of a circular tray resting on the head and raised hands of a bearded term (QG, 1974–5, No.2; Jagger, pp.110–12).

121 Head of a laughing Child (? Henry VIII)
attributed to Guido Mazzoni, c.1500
COLOUR PLATE XXII facing page 113

Life-size terracotta bust of a laughing boy looking to his right. The face and neck are painted in naturalistic colours; the eyes are blue. On his head is a tight-fitting gold net cap with red visible in the interstices. He is dressed in a brocade tunic of raised wax decoration overlaid with gold and silver leaf glazed with green, red and yellow. The tunic, open at the neck, reveals a pleated white shirt below a gold band. Height, $12\frac{1}{2}$ in. (31.8 cm); width, $13\frac{1}{2}$ in. (34.3 cm); depth, 6 in. (15.2 cm)

The attribution of the bust to Guido Mazzoni (died 1518) was first made in 1960 by Helen J. Dow ('Two Italian Portrait-Busts of Henry VIII', *The Art Bulletin*, No.42 (New York, December 1960), pp.291–4). She argues convincingly that it is very probably a portrait of Henry VIII at the age of about eight commissioned by his father.

Mazzoni had attracted the attention of Charles VIII of France during his disastrous invasion on Italy in 1495. The King prevailed on Mazzoni to accompany him back to France, where Louis XII later commissioned him to execute Charles VIII's tomb in St Denis (it was destroyed during the Revolution). Louis XII's influence inspired Henry VII to order his own tomb at Westminster Abbey from Mazzoni: a commission eventually executed by Torrigiano.

The realistic representation of the laughing countenance of the child with parted lips and sideways glance are characteristic of Mazzoni's style. As Helen Dow aptly remarks 'the mischievous charm of a happy little boy radiates from every detail'.

The recent analysis and conservation of the bust by J.H. Larson has revealed the high standard of craftsmanship involved in its creation – the average thickness of the clay is less than 1 cm compared to 3–4 cm in the case of the majority of other terracottas of this period. The finely applied flesh tones are original. The hair net has been regilded; the black overpaint of the tunic conceals a much more sophisticated form of decoration incorporating raised patterns of transparent glazes of colour over silver, gold or tin leaf.[1]

The history of the bust prior to the nineteenth century remains uncertain. The first documented mention of it is an entry by Benjamin Jutsham dated 4 September 1815 in the Carlton House Deliveries Ledger, which records the despatch to Brighton of 'The Cast of a Chinese Boy's Head. Laughing Countenance'. It would be easy to mistake the head, with its narrowed eyes, for that of a Chinaman.

[1] We are indebted to Mr Larson for the technical information published in this entry.

122 Antiope and Theseus(?) by Adriaen de Vries, c.1610–15

Bronze group, with an even grey-brown patina. A naked male figure, supported by a stunted tree rising from between his feet, strides across an oval base treated naturalistically. He gazes up at a naked female figure whom he clasps in his arms. She returns his gaze and points upwards with her left hand while in her right she holds a bow. Height, $37\frac{1}{2}$ in. (95.2 cm); width, $14\frac{1}{2}$ in. (36.8 cm); depth, 14 in. (35.6 cm). Signed with the monogram *AF*.

This group was not discussed by L.O. Larsson in his study of the sculptor (*Adriaen de Vries*...(Vienna, 1967)), as he evidently did not know of its existence. Eva Zimmermann considers it in the context of a bronze group of Hercules, Diana and Nessus in the Badisches Landesmuseum. Its composition is very similar to that of the bronze in the Royal Collection, but with the addition of a fallen Nessus over whom Hercules strides. She dates the three-figure group, of which other examples are known, to 1603, soon after de Vries had been appointed sculptor to Rudolph II in Prague. For reasons which are not entirely clear she suggests that the two-figure group may date from *c*.1610–15 ('Herkules, Deianeira und Nessus', *Jahrbuch des Staatlichen Kunstsammlungen in Baden-Württemberg*, vol.VI (1969), pp.55–78).

Though the group has traditionally been described as Diana abducted by Antaeus, it seems more likely, as first suggested by Eva Zimmermann, that it represents Theseus carrying off the queen of the Amazons, Antiope.

122

123

124

123 Spring by Massimiliano Soldani-Benzi, 1715

Bronze relief, with an even brownish-black patina. Seated on the right is the goddess Flora accompanied by Vertumnus and Pomona. To the left putti and nymphs are bedecking a herm with garlands of flowers. In the background wild half-naked figures dance round a flaming brazier. Surveying the scene from above are Jupiter and Juno seated on a cloud. 19 in. (48.2 cm) × 26$\frac{1}{8}$ in. (66.3 cm). Signed and dated 1715. Inscribed on a parchment which a putti is reading: *BURLINGTONVS eris:/Manibus date lilia plenis:/Purpureos spargam/flores:* (translated literally: You will be Burlington: Give lilies with full hands: I shall scatter scarlet flowers).

This relief, together with the three others, of Summer, Autumn and Winter (Nos.123–5), belonged to Lord Burlington (1694–1753) who may have ordered them when he was in Florence on the Grand Tour in 1715, as suggested by Pamela D. Kingsbury (letter dated 10 March 1981). On the evidence of an inventory (*c.*1870) of the sculpture in Windsor Castle, 'Lord Burleigh' (presumably an error for Lord Burlington) presented them to George II. They were hung in Kensington Palace.

Three sets of bronzes of this composition are known. Massimiliano Soldani-Benzi (1656–1740) was first commissioned by Crown Prince Ferdinando de' Medici to cast two plaques, representing Summer and Autumn, for presentation in 1708 to his brother-in-law, Johann-Wilhelm, the Elector-Palatine. Two further plaques, allegorical of Spring and Winter and completing the series, were despatched three years later. The set is now preserved in the Bayerisches Nationalmuseum. A third set, of two plaques only, comprising Summer and Autumn, which were acquired in 1955 by the University of Kansas, may be related to the pair which are recorded in 1761 in the possession of Sampson Gideon of Belvedere House, Erith, Kent (information supplied by Kathryn M. Delaney citing *London and its Environs Described* (1761), vol.I, p.274).

In addition to the bronze reliefs the original terracotta models survive. Crown Prince Ferdinando had them framed and glazed and hung in his audience chambers. They are now in the Pitti Palace, Florence. A set in Doccia porcelain slightly reduced in scale (42 × 59 cm) was also produced (sold Christie's, Hôtel Richemond, Geneva, 2 October 1969 (91)).

Like the terracotta reliefs the bronze plaques were originally framed – the original set retains its heavy moulded ebony frames which set off to advantage the bronzes with their golden brown patina – and were intended to hang on walls like paintings in a gallery. Lankheit, who illustrates an engraving published in 1778 of the Elector's Gallery in Düsseldorf in which the reliefs are shown hanging next to paintings, suggests that this may be the first example of bronze reliefs being treated as movable objects rather than as fixed decorative panels forming part of an architectural scheme (Lankheit, pp.1–9).

The Royal Collection set was also framed. On 2 April 1814 B.L. Vulliamy rebronzed the reliefs at a cost of five guineas each. He also supplied mahogany backboards and strong glazed ebony frames for a total cost of £84 (PRO, C104/58, No.34, p.477; LC/11/17) (see Bayerisches Nationalmuseum, Munich, *Catalogue*, vol.XIII, 5, H.R. Weihrauch, 'Die Bildwerke in Bronze . . .' (Munich, 1956) pp.172–6; K. Lankheit, 'Two Bronze Reliefs by Massimiliano Soldani-Benzi', *The Register of the Museum of Art of the University of Kansas*, No.9 (Dec. 1957) pp.1–9)).

124 Summer by Massimiliano Soldani-Benzi, 1715

Bronze relief, with an even brownish-black patina. On the left Triptolemus drives a chariot drawn by two dragons in which Ceres is seated. By the chariot stands a nymph with a sieve, personifying vegetation. Advancing from the right is a procession of figures bearing agricultural implements (rake, fork, plough, sickle, flail, hoe etc.) and leading a team of oxen. 19 in. (48.3 cm) × 26$\frac{1}{8}$ in. (66.3 cm). Signed and dated 1715. See No.123.

125

126

126

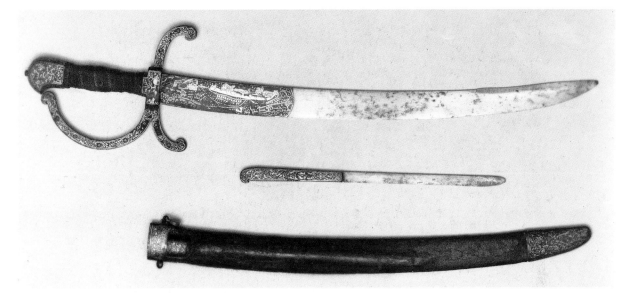

127

125 Autumn by Massimiliano Soldani-Benzi, 1715

Bronze relief, with an even brownish-black patina. On the left a drunken Silenus is supported by two companions as he balances precariously on a donkey. Around him dance satyrs, maenads and bacchantes. On the right Bacchus reclines beside Ariadne, while behind them putti, brandishing thyrsi and masks, play around the god's chariot from which the leopards have been unharnessed. $18\frac{3}{4}$ in. (47.6 cm) × $26\frac{1}{8}$ in. (66.3 cm). Signed and dated 1715. See No.123.

126 Winter by Massimiliano Soldani-Benzi, 1715

Bronze relief, with an even brownish-black patina. Mars and Venus are shown on the left arriving at the entrance to Vulcan's forge. The goddess's chariot from which she has just stepped, drawn by doves and swans, is on the left. Behind them are the three Graces. To the right Vulcan sits holding a shield inscribed *Unum omnia contra tela* (one weapon against all weapons), while behind him in the cave Cyclopes labour at the forge. In the top right-hand corner is a shield bearing Lord Burlington's arms (Per bend crennellé argent and gules). $19\frac{1}{8}$ in. (48.6 cm) × 26 in. (66 cm). Signed and dated 1715. See No.123.

127 Hunting Sword by Diego de Çaias, 1544

The iron hilt consists of an asymmetrical 'bird's head' pommel and a pair of quillons (cross-guards) supporting a knuckle-guard. The baluster-shaped wooden grip, probably an eighteenth-century replacement, is bound with a variety of twists of iron and gold wire, and has Turk's head ferrules. The short, single-edged, curved blade has a shamfre for 6 in. (15.2 cm), from the tip. The outer face of the blade near the hilt is counterfeit-damascened with a scene representing the siege of a city with a waggon park on the left. The inner face inscribed in Roman capitals: *HENRICI OCTAVI|LETARE BOLONIA|DVCTV PVRPVREIS|TVRRES CONSPICIE|NDA ROSIS IAM|TRACTA IACEN* [sic]*|MALE OLENTIA| LILIA PVLSVS G|ALLVS ET INVI[C]TA| REGNAT IN ARCE|LEO SIC TIBI NEC|VIRT[V]S DEERIT|NE[C] [GR]ATIA FOR|MAE [CV]M LEO|TVTELA CVM|ROSA[S]IT DECORI*

The wooden scabbard is covered in black leather of eighteenth-century date and has a top-locket and chape, the former with a fixed ring on each side for suspension, and a pocket for a byeknife with a haft matching the guards and a single-edged slightly curved blade with a round tip. The decoration of the metalwork is by means of counterfeit-damascening against a russetted ground (probably originally blued). Length overall, $25\frac{3}{4}$ in. (65.4 cm); length of blade, $19\frac{3}{4}$ in. (50.2 cm).

Made for Henry VIII; recorded in 1798 in George Wallis's private museum, Hull; subsequently in the collections of the Earl of Londesborough (sold Christie's, 4 July etc., 1888 (172)), F. Spitzer (sold Paris, 10–14 June 1895 (212)) and the Princes Odescalchi. Acquired for the Royal Collection in 1966.

The scene on the blade, as Claude Blair has demonstrated, is a realistic representation of the siege of Boulogne by the English army under Henry VIII in the late summer of 1544. The wording of the inscription on the other face of the blade indicates that this weapon was decorated shortly after the capitulation of the town on 14 September.

The style of the decoration is so similar to that of a number of weapons, in other collections, signed by Diego de Çaias, a Spanish workman known to have been in the service of Henry VIII and Edward VI between 1542/3 and 1549, if not later, that Blair felt able to attribute this weapon to him also. An entry in the 1547 Royal Inventory might actually refer to it. It includes 'two longs Woodknives . . . of Diego his makinge . . . euerie of them Havinge skaberde of vellut knives and Bodkin' (C. Blair, 'A Royal Swordsmith and Damascener, Diego de Çaias', *Metropolitan Museum Journal*, vol.III (1970), pp.149–98, particularly pp.166–72, figs.30–35.)

128 Cup-hilt Rapier and left hand-Dagger, German, (?)Italian and (?)Spanish, seventeenth and eighteenth centuries

The rapier with iron hilt, consisting of a writhen and chiselled pommel supporting a knuckle-guard, a pair of arms, and a solid cup-shaped guard. Inside the cup is a circular dust-guard (*guardapolvo*) made of two concentric plates. The wooden spirally-bound grip has eight longitudinal, knurled bars and a pair of writhen ferrules of iron. The associated straight two-edged blade of flattened hexagonal section. The ricasso (slightly lengthened) is struck on the outside with an illegible mark. The short central fuller is etched on each side: *HEINRICH COELL MEFECIT SOLINGEN.*

The dagger with hilt consisting of an identical but smaller pommel, straight quillons with a triangular knuckle-guard and decoration and grip matching that of the rapier. The straight two-edged blade with a broad ricasso $4\frac{3}{4}$ in. (12.1 cm) long, with bevelled edges and two holes and two prongs. On the outer face between the holes is struck an unidentified maker's mark, a flaming star. Length overall of the rapier, 46 in. (116.8 cm); length of blade, 39 in. (99 cm); length overall of the dagger, $22\frac{3}{8}$ in. (57 cm); length of blade, $17\frac{1}{2}$ in. (44.5 cm).

Listed in the Carlton House Catalogue, Nos.2309 and 2310, where they are said to have come from the armoury of Don Manuel de Godoy, Prince of Peace (1767–1851), and to have been given to the Prince Regent in 1812 by General Doyle.

The hilts are probably Italian (Milanese) third quarter of the seventeenth century, the blade of the sword German (Solingen) probably eighteenth-century and the blade of the dagger possibly Spanish, third quarter of the seventeenth century. A rather similar hilt in the Metropolitan Museum of Art, New York (Acc. No.11.89.2), is signed by Carlo Picinino. This otherwise unknown maker was presumably one of the well-known Milanese family of armourers and bladesmiths.

Four bladesmiths called Heinrich Kohl or Koehl are recorded in Solingen in the seventeenth and eighteenth century (Laking, Nos.67 and 68; A.V.B. Norman & C.M. Barne, *The Rapier*, 1980, p.178).

129 Parade Mace, possibly Italian second half of the sixteenth century

The head is made of a single piece of grey and rose agate pierced longitudinally for the iron haft. It has eight flanges and is diamond-shaped in profile, and the grey agate grip is octagonal. The iron is richly counterfeit-damascened in gold against a russet ground. Length, $20\frac{7}{8}$ in. (53 cm).

Traditionally called the sceptre of Elizabeth, Queen of Bohemia (1596–1662), and thought to have been bequeathed by her to William, Lord Craven. Thence by descent in the Craven and Keppel families to the late Earl of Albemarle by whom given to The Queen in 1978.

Though the form is that of a fighting-mace of the period, the delicate decoration, and especially the agate head, indicates that it was intended merely for show. A related mace, the so-called sceptre of Charlemagne, formerly in the Abbey of Werden and now in Berlin, was exhibited in *Karl der Grosse*, Aachen, 1965 cat. no.676. Another, of jasper and silver-gilt, from the Church of Teisendorf Oberbayern, is in the Bayerisches Nationalmuseum (W.1625).

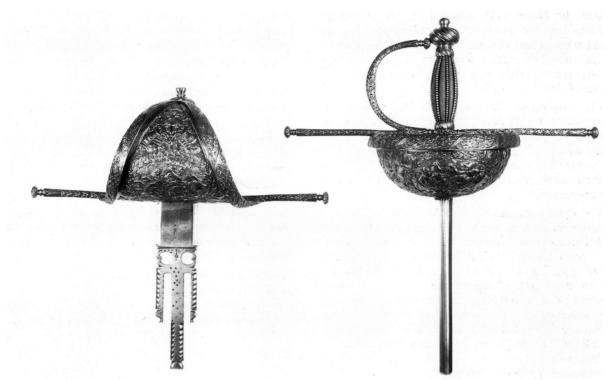

128

129

130

130 Small-Sword, hilt probably Paris c.1655

The iron hilt, with vase-shaped pommel, prominent tang-button, a sleeve with a pair of short quillons (cross guards), diminutive arms of the hilt, and a pair of asymmetrical shells made in one piece. The iron crisply chiselled all over, and pierced in places, with minute military scenes, the figures in classical dress and armour. The later wooden grip spirally bound with iron wire and with Turk's head ferrules. The associated blade is straight and two-edged, and near the hilt is etched in line with tightly scrolled foliage. Length overall, $39\frac{15}{16}$ in. (101.5 cm); length of blade, $32\frac{15}{16}$ in. (83.7 cm).

Bought by George IV from Bland, 4 March 1789, for £26. 15s., and listed in the Carlton House Catalogue, No.272, where it is said to have been given to John Churchill, 1st Duke of Marlborough (1650–1722), by the Emperor Charles VI (1711–40).

Laking compared the workmanship of this hilt with that of the two swords in the old Royal Armoury in Stockholm. These are now thought to have been bought in Paris for the coronation of Carl X Gustav in 1654. Presumably the decoration of these hilts was carried out by one of the *fourbisseurs* or medallists who had *logements* in the *Galeries du Louvre* at this period (Norman & Barne, op. cit., p.200).

At the time when the alleged presentation to Marlborough took place, this hilt would probably have had considerable value as a curiosity. A similar hilt is illustrated in a picture entitled *The antiques dealer* by Jan de Herdt, dated 1662 (Karlsruhe, Staatl. Kunsthalle, Inv. No.189) (Laking, No.59; Norman & Barne, op. cit., pp.200 and 382, pl.99).

131 Round Target, Paris or Antwerp, mid-sixteenth century

COLOUR PLATE XXIII (detail) facing page 132

The shield is of iron, concave towards the body, with a rolled turn along the edge, and with a three-piece central boss with a conical spike, decorated with concentric circles, the outer one inscribed in gold with silver capitals all in counterfeit-damascening: *AMBITVS HIC MINIMVS MAGNAM CAPIT AMBITIONEM,/QVAE REGNA EVERTIT DESTRVIT IMPERIA./SVSTVLIT E MEDIO MAGNI VITAMQVE DECVSQVE/POMPEII EVEXIT CAESARIS IMPERIVM./CAESARIS IN*

131

COELVM MITIS CLEMENTIA FERTVR,/QVAE TAMEN HVIC TANDEM PERNICIOSA FVIT./ANNVLVS EXIT EI LACHRYMAS CERVIXQVE RESECTA/POMPEII HINC PATVIT QVAM PROBVS ILLE FORET./IN SACRIS DOCVIT VESTIS CONSPERSA CRVORE/HVIC PRAESAGA MALI TALIA FATA FORE./SI VIRES IGITVR SPECTAVENS [sic] *AMBITIONIS/NON GRAVIVS VIDEAS AMBITIONE MALVM/* and with a series of embossed ovals representing scenes apparently from the life of Julius Caesar: the presentation of Pompey's head to Caesar; the incident of the defilement of Caesar's robe by the blood of the sacrifice; and two battle scenes, one with the death of a leader. Diameter, 23 in. (58.5 cm).

This shield is one of the finest examples of a group of embossed parade armour made for the French court in the middle years of the sixteenth century. Dr Bruno Thomas published all the known pieces as well as the many surviving designs for them (Vienna *Jahrbuch*, vol.LV (1959), pp.31–74; *idem*, vol.LVI (1960), pp.7–26; *idem*, vol.LVIII (1962), pp.101–68; *idem*, vol.LXI (1965), pp.41–90). These drawings are attributed to Etienne Delaune (1518/19–83), who is known to have been working for Henri II between 1552 and the King's death in 1559.

It is not clear whether this group of armour was actually made in France, or in Antwerp by the goldsmith Eliseus Libaerts, who is known to have made or decorated a group of very similar pieces for Erik XIV of Sweden about 1561–63. The greater part of Libaerts's armour for the Swedish King survives, divided between Stockholm and Dresden (C. Blair, *The James A. de Rothschild Collection at Waddesdon Manor, Arms and Armour and Base Metalwork* (Fribourg, 1974), Cat. No.9).

Dr Thomas has suggested that this shield was made for Henri II (1547–59) on the grounds that the style and theme of its decoration echo those of his armour now in the Musée du Louvre and that a very similar shield exists or existed bearing the King's monogram ('Die Münchner Waffenvorzeichnungen des Étienne Delaune und die Prunkschilde Heinrichs II. von Frankreich', Vienna *Jahrbruch*, vol.LVIII (1962), pp.101–68 particularly pp.144–5, and fig.124) (Laking, No.71).

PLATE XXIII
Detail from a round Target (No.131)

Overleaf:

PLATE XXIV
Four-sided astronomical Clock by Christopher Pinchbeck and others (No.120)